A nostalgic look at

BLACKPOOL TRAMS

1950-1966

Steve Palmer

Silver Link Publishing Ltd

BLACKPOOL TRAMS 1950-1966

CONTENTS

Title page Here we are on a sunny day looking at the view through the raised windscreen of the new twin-cars 276-275, starting the 1958 Coastal Tour. Approaching Standard 147 is passing the 'Wonderland of the World' and about to reach an advertisement for the Coastal Tour, a rival! We can sample the attractions within the building upon the facade: Charles Barlow & The Tower Band in the Ballroom; Lions, Tigers, Bears and Leopards in the Menagerie; and Charlie Cairoli will make you laugh in the Circus! On a sunny day a tour along the coast by tram provides interesting sea-views of Morecambe Bay towards the Lake District. Everybody is nicely dressed in this Fifties view - men wearing jackets and ties, while ladies have matching dresses.

By the way, if you were here in the morning you could see a procession of elephants from the Circus stables going for exercise on the beach with their trainers. It is remembered how an elephant once fancied a rest upon a parked red Mini car - and squashed it flat. Beware! *R. P. Fergusson*

Opposite page A delightful scene, also in the Fifties, on the Central Promenade, with railcoaches in their striking livery dominated by the 520-foot Tower of 1894. The imposing row of buildings includes the County Hotel at the corner of Church Street, the noble facade of The Palace, including Theatre, Cinema and Ballroom, the 'Wonderland of the World', containing the Circus, Ballroom with Wurlitzer, Aquarium and Menagerie, and the Woolworths building of the Thirties. Work is under way painting the Tower from top to bottom, shown by the scaffolding platforms. There is a breeze from the sea, shown by the clothes of the walkers along the Promenade, and the sun is shining through the clouds.

The Palace was opened as the Alhambra in 1899, bought by the Tower Company and renamed and re-opened in July 1904. In March 1961 it was announced that the Palace and the County Hotel had been were bought by Lewis's, who demolished them and by 1963 had built a multi-storey emporium. In its last season Frankie Vaughan starred in the Palace of Varieties, while the Cinema showed the epic *Ben Hur*. This was one of the greatest entertainment centres in the North of England; replaced by Lewis's, it has now been reconstructed to house Mecca Bingo, Woolworths and Harry Ramsden's chip restaurant. The majority wish that The Palace had been listed for preservation and was still keeping the Tower company to this day! *Author's collection*

First published in April 1995

British Library Cataloguing in Publication Data

A catalogue record for this book is available from the British Library.

ISBN 1 85794 041 5

Silver Link Publishing Ltd
Unit 5
Home Farm Close
Church Street
Wadenhoe
Peterborough PE8 5TE
Tel/fax (01832) 720440

Printed and bound in Great Britain

AUTHOR'S PREFACE AND ACKNOWLEDGEMENTS

THE Blackpool Tramway is now celebrating its 110th birthday, a remarkable survival in Britain when other city tramways have long since passed away, concluding with Glasgow in 1962. This book takes a nostalgic look at the famous years of the Fifties and Sixties when the trams operated in many parts of the town - and the public enjoyed them! Naturally the trams were picturesque in a variety of identities, including the illuminated trams and the vintage trams for the 75th Anniversary in 1960. However, upon the demise of the street tramways in the early Sixties, preservation secured the survival of 22 Blackpool trams elsewhere in Britain and the USA. Consequently you can still share with myself the enjoyment of the Blackpool Trams,

which for me started in my childhood, and remains to this day.

I would like to thank my fellow tramway enthusiasts who have shared their photographs with me to illustrate this book: Dennis Gill, Robert Fergusson, David Packer, Geoff Hyde and Graham Weaver. I am grateful for the assistance of Ian McLoughlin, Terry Daniel, Colin Macleod, Graham Twidale and John Fozard. I pay tribute to those who have supported me: Tony Depledge (Managing Director of Blackpool Transport Services), Barry Morris (Director of Tourism Services, Blackpool Borough Council) and Peter Horsley (Maritime, Commercial & Industrial Photography of Fleetwood); and finally for the assistance of the *Evening Gazette,* Blackpool. Hold tight! We're off!

A splendid view from Bispham, looking north along the coast to Rossall Point, showing Coronation 324 in service - this tram is still with us today. This location shows the delightful path for a walk along the cliff-top, with the bench seats and traditional shelters for relaxation. Following the opening of the tramroad in 1898, and the recruiting of Bispham with Norbreck UDC to Blackpool in 1917, the Promenade has developed with the **growth of property including hotels. The towers of the Norbreck Hydro Hotel are outstanding in their size and appearance, and along the coast you can see Queens Theatre at Cleveleys, Rossall Public School and the Cinderella Home at Rossall. When you have walked along Cliff-top you can cross the tramroad by a neat footpath to the Methodist Church, whose sign says 'Always Welcome'.** *Saidman Brothers, Ian McLoughlin Collection*

FOREWORD

Sir Stanley Matthews

IN 1955, when I was playing for Blackpool, I was intended to be the very first 'victim' of a new BBC TV programme, *This Is Your Life*. In the event the surprise plot didn't work - a daily newspaper gave the game away - and it was to be 1969 before Eamonn Andrews caught me with the Big Red Book. And in a way looking through these photographs of Blackpool and its trams in that era has been rather like meeting once again an old friend of 40 years ago.

I was stationed in Blackpool for a few months during the War and used the trams frequently. Later, between 1947 and 1961, I lived and played in Blackpool, but by then I had a car and used the trams less frequently. However, whenever we had friends visiting us we would take them for a ride on one, as a traditional Blackpool treat! And of course the football supporters used to travel to Bloomfield Road by bus and tram Specials showing 'Football Ground' on their indicators.

I've always been fascinated by trams. As a lad in Hanley I was always jumping on a tram - you never sat down, just hung on, a ring on the bell and you were off. They were a way of life, cheap and convenient. I used to holiday on the Isle of Man and loved the trams there, too. Then 20 years ago I was coaching in San Francisco, and rode the city's streetcars. I didn't realise until looking at these photographs that since 1985 there's been a Blackpool Boat car there, too!

For me Blackpool's Promenade trams are the finest in the world. No traffic to dodge when you get on and off - just the wide open Prom, the beach and the sea. What pleasant memories the photographs bring back of my happy years in the

Evening Gazette, Blackpool

town, in an era when life seems to me to have been altogether better ordered and more disciplined than it is today, in everyday life as well as on the football pitch!

I lived then near Lytham Road, which features in a number of the photographs. I used to drop my young son off at Arnold School (he now runs a large tennis complex in Connecticut, USA!), drive up to Squires Gate, where the trams turned, leave the car and do 45 minutes' training on the beach before going to the ground. If passengers were boarding or leaving trams in the middle of the road, as a motorist you had to wait! It wouldn't be allowed today - the modern tramway systems such as that in Manchester have to be more segregated than the old systems were, when they were so much a part of the street scene.

When I wasn't working I was lucky enough to get to know many of Blackpool's Summer Season celebrities, and through such organisations as the Water Rats I had great fun taking part in charity sporting events, golf, football and so on. There were so many good friends - Ted Ray, Nat Jackley, Max Bygraves, Henry Hall, Wee Georgie Wood, my old friend Charlie Chester, Tommy Cooper - we had to fit studs to his shoes because we hadn't any size 12 football boots!

Perhaps most memorable of all were the illuminated trams. In 1951 I was asked to switch on the Illuminations; the ceremony was followed by a tour round the Lights by tram - a great occasion. Happily the Promenade trams - and the Illuminations - are still very much with us, giving Blackpool that unique quality that I enjoyed so much in the 1950s, and have been able to relive again in this wonderfully evocative collection of photographs.

In 1963 the Promenade tramway is as busy as ever! In the foreground are the boats on wheels waiting to be launched into the sea by truck, to provide sailings along the coast for a view of the landscape. There is a happy feeling of good weather - bare arms getting sunburned! Looking along the famous line of buildings we see the Palatine Hotel, Woolworths, the Tower - but the absence of the Palace, being replaced by the construction of the new Lewis's store in Sixties style. *Author*

BLACKPOOL TRAMS 1950-1966

CENTRAL PROMENADE, SOUTH SHORE AND SQUIRES GATE

BLACKPOOL'S claim to fame was established by Michael Holroyd Smith, founder of the tramway, who said: 'This line will be the first in the world to be worked safely in the public street by electricity'. A conduit street tramway was laid along the Promenade between North Pier and Victoria Pier, and opened on 29 September 1885: '. . .and other seaside towns will follow the good example'.

The trams drew their power from a conduit groove between the rails, using a plough. While providing a sensational ride, problems arose from flooding by high tides and the blocking of the centre groove with sand. This sometimes halted electric traction, and led to horses drawing the trams. However, a new route on the conduit system was built along Lytham Road to South Station in 1895, although the track continued to Squires Gate and was used by a horse tram. In 1896 this was replaced by gas trams operated by the Blackpool, St Annes & Lytham Tramway Company, starting from South Shore Station. In the same year the final conduit track was built along Station Road, which linked the Promenade with Lytham Road. Suffice to say that a decision was made in 1898 to convert the conduit to the overhead line system, used to this day. The trams sported trolleys, and the overhead wire was suspended by bracket-arms on traction poles along the Promenade, giving them distinction as street lights too.

In 1900 the tramway was extended to the north through Claremont Park to Gynn Square, where it met the Blackpool & Fleetwood Tramroad giving rides along the coast. New open-toppers - called the Dreadnoughts - were introduced, and were unique with their full-width steps and twin staircases. The popularity of both tramways was thus developed by the changing of trams at Gynn Square from a Dreadnought to the inter-urban single-deck cars. Meanwhile, at South Shore a fairground had commenced in the Nineties and in 1906 was named The Pleasure Beach by its founder, W. G. Bean. Today it is still owned by his Thompson family, and The Pleasure Beach and the trams continue to depend mutually upon each other.

It is worthy of note that between 1902 and 1905 the Promenade was widened to 100 feet and the tramway re-sited on a reservation with a private right-of-way. Meanwhile, on Lytham Road the gas trams were replaced in 1903 by electric trams of the same Company. In 1909, when an Air Display took place at Squires Gate, Blackpool's trams joined in operation along the full length of Lytham Road. The Squires Gate route was then operated by Blackpool from Gynn Square, while the Lytham blue-cars started at Central Station.

In 1920 the Blackpool & Fleetwood Company was taken over by the Borough, and the track was connected at Gynn Square and North Station. The North Shore Promenade track was re-sited on a reservation above the new Middle Walk in 1923, and in the following year an elaborate track layout was built at Gynn Square. It was then possible for Blackpool

trams to operate to the Cabin, and by 1926 as far as Bispham. In the same year the Lytham blue-cars reached a new northern terminus at Gynn Square, and here the three distinctive tramways met.

In 1926, at South Shore, there was a proposal to extend the Promenade to Clifton Drive, securing the right-of-way past the Pleasure Beach in return for a concession. All trams travelling beyond that point must now show SOUTH PROMENADE via PLEASURE BEACH on the indicator, so that passengers cannot forget it! This new Promenade had a reserved-track tramway, sunken gardens and a paddling pool

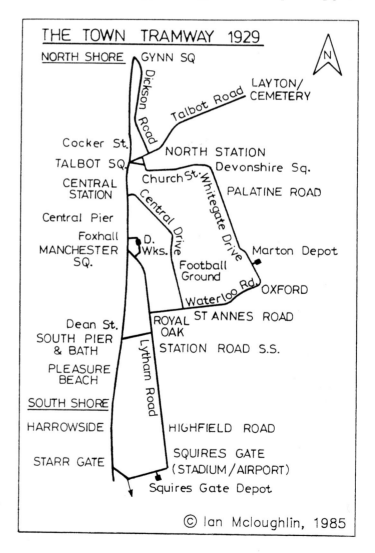

Tramways in Blackpool town in 1929. 'D. Wks.' = Rigby Road Depot and Works. *Ian McLoughlin*

at Harrowside. Development of new hotels in impressive terraces took place, which created the need for a regular service to Fleetwood. Blue-cars then gained their rights of access to the Promenade, and travelled alternately via Lytham Road to Gynn Square. In the height of the season, short-workings turned at Harrowside from the Cabin.

The coastal route from Starr Gate to Fleetwood was now 11 miles long - and remains so to this day. If only Blackpool had acquired the Lytham St Annes tramway in 1937, it was intended to extend the Promenade tramway reservation to St Annes Square. Unfortunately they lost the chance of a longer coastal line by the casting vote of the Lytham St Annes Mayor, but it would have been wonderful today!

During the Thirties the Modernisation Plan of General Manager Walter Luff introduced 116 streamlined trams. These comprised 45 railcoaches for the coastal routes, 12 open Boat cars for Circulars, 13 'Luxury Dreadnoughts' for the Promenade, 14 double-deck Balloons for the Squires Gate route, and 12 sun-saloon cars, all built by the English Electric Company at Preston. Additionally 20 railcars were built by Brush of Loughborough, and compensated for the loss of the neighbouring blue-cars in 1937. Thus they began the Squires Gate and Fleetwood service, and later transferred to Bispham Depot in 1940 for Service 1, North Station and Fleetwood.

This famous fleet of streamliners had centre-entrance saloons, comfortable cushioned seats, sliding sunshine roofs, electric clocks and heaters. Passengers liked them so much that they were prepared to let old trams pass by, and travel on the new ones: 'We don't want to ride on the old 'uns, when there's them posh 'uns about.' When they boarded, passengers looked for a mat to wipe their feet, and men removed their hats indoors! This new generation of the fleet provided the trams with popularity and prestige on the transport scene.

While considerable effort went into relaying the track of the Promenade and Fleetwood route, including turning loops at Little Bispham, Pleasure Beach and Starr Gate, in 1936 a decision was made also to relay the Lytham Road street track. It is interesting to record that the proposal included building central islands between the tracks, which would facilitate off-side loading of passengers with safety. One of the new Brush cars with driver-operated power doors had an unfortunate experience on Lytham Road. When the driver opened the off-side doors by mistake, all the luggage carried on its centre platform cascaded into the path of a following bus! Suffice to say that in 1938 the new Lytham Road track did get relaid in the same position without islands - and conductors operated the power-doors themselves!

The Airport at Squires Gate made the tram route very busy during the War. Here was situated the large Vickers-Armstrong factory that manufactured the Wellington bombers and employed 10,000 workers. There was a proposal for an extension eastwards along Squires Gate Lane to the factory gates, but this was not to materialise because of the cost. The surviving tracks between Squires Gate and Starr Gate,

Central Promenade

A Central Promenade scene with the Golden Mile, the Tower and a handsome Coronation car of 1953, bound for 'South Promenade via Pleasure Beach'. On the beach many people are enjoying relaxing in their deckchairs, children making their sandcastles, while others visit the caravans selling tea or ice-cream. A few people stroll along the Promenade, while more are on the other side of the road visiting the attractions of the Golden Mile. Here there are a variety of entertainments, including the Super Dodgems and the Ghost Train. In the Fifties many trippers come by train or coach, but some were beginning to come by car - some are seen parked along the carriageway. *Valentine & Sons, Dundee*

belonging to Lytham St Annes, was retained for tram dispersal to their depot in an air-raid, if necessary.

During the post-war years, in 1957, this track came into use again with the re-introduction of the Circular Tour. During the Fifties a five-minute service from Squires Gate during the season was alternated between double-deckers to Cabin and single-deckers to Bispham. Upon the Promenade a similar schedule of service alternated from Starr Gate between Thornton Gate and Fleetwood, and both used rail-coaches. It was sensational when 25 new Coronation cars were introduced in 1952-4 and took over the service. Although appropriately named after the Royal occasion in 1953, they were nicknamed 'Spivs' by the staff. With fast acceleration and smooth running, the Coronations were popular with both residents and holidaymakers, but were expensive to operate with heavy power consumption. Drivers claimed that they were 'catching the seagulls' on the Coronations, but many trams were halted by power-cuts. Accordingly the new lively trams had their performance in

acceleration reduced! Although still looking handsome in service, by 1975 they had been withdrawn and replaced by a more economical generation of OMOs.

By 1958 there was need for track renewal of the Squires Gate route, and work commenced during the winter on relaying the Royal Oak junction. During this time buses were used along Lytham Road instead of trams, and this provided an indication of cost savings in not relaying the whole street route. In October 1960, just after the 75th Anniversary procession along the Promenade in Blackpool, and the last tram in Sheffield, the decision was taken to close the route. Therefore Blackpool joined the other deprived cities, when on 29 October 1961 railcoach 268 left Squires Gate for the last time. On the next day bus operation of route 12 by Blackpool Transport joined the blue-buses that had been running on Lytham Road since 1937. There were no more Circular Tours and Marton trams to South Pier, but the Promenade trams continue in service to this day - on their 110th Anniversary in 1995!

Coronation car 322, destined for Starr Gate, passes the 'Measured Mile' post, which could be used by the police to clock the speed of the motorists. It is true that the police also clocked the speed of the powerful Coronations - sometimes exceeding 30 mph. This August 1963 scene sees the approach of the Autumn Illuminations; the tram is passing 'Snow White and the Seven Dwarfs'. Thousands of people stroll along the seafront, while others cross the carriageway towards the Golden Mile and Dutton Ales at the Victoria Arms. *Author*

ALL CARS STOP HERE - if you want a tram to the Tower - but these passengers want to ride further, and 247 leaves them behind. Here at Central Pier we can see on the extreme left the 1937 Lifeboat House opposite Louis Tussaud's Waxworks, one of the many attractions of the Golden Mile. When the tram reaches the Tower the duty Inspector will decide upon its destination according to queues. Trams like 247 were 'specials' between service cars, and frequently changed their destinations upon demand. *Author*

South Shore

Alexandra Road is a tram-stop identified by the nautical rigging of the flag mast here. This elevated viewpoint illustrates the wide Promenade, which provides the ideal tramway reservation free from traffic, and a wonderful clear space for strollers. The carriageway is lined with many parked cars on both sides, while a Riley saloon drives towards the Pleasure Beach. The Coronation tram can be distinguished by its narrow roof, lined by windows and curved roof lights, providing a sunny ride for the passengers. Decorating the tram's dash panel beneath the windscreen are the chrome streamlines on each side of the inverted triangle - an exclusive style on a unique type of tram. *Valentine & Sons, Dundee*

On 17 August 1958 Coronation car 317, destined for Thornton Gate via Cleveleys, is parked upon the Pleasure Beach siding, having broken down. While it looks clean and tidy, it may have been subject to brake failure when the Vambac accelerator jammed. This rotary contact arm could become isolated by blowing sand entering through the ventilator grill. Certainly this was a problem with its location in the roof, compared with similar accelerators on USA PCC cars, where it was beneath the floor. The seaside provides unusual hazards to certain susceptible trams, like the 1885 conduit cars as well as the more modern Coronations. Incidentally, the other trams are waiting for passengers, and the Balloon may have taken over the service. *A. D. Packer*

In August 1994 the South Promenade scene is dominated by the new Giant Roller Coaster, introduced to the Pleasure Beach in that year. Balloon 712 on the service to Fleetwood loads opposite The Star public house, built in 1932. The lamp-post-mounted Santa again draws our attention to the Illuminations to come, in company with Marilyn Monroe, Elvis Presley and Groucho Marx! *Author*

BLACKPOOL TRAMS 1950-1966

Squires Gate

Above At Starr Gate, seen here on 23 May 1959, trams could leave the Promenade reservation and travel along Squires Gate Lane, formerly used by the Lytham St Annes blue-cars until 1937. Blackpool continued to operate Circular Tours on this route until 1961, while here is seen Balloon 244 on a special tour for Light Rail Transport League members. This will be a nostalgic recollection for those who took part; however, Promenade trams still return on the loop line to this day. *Author*

Below Travelling along Squires Gate Lane on the same day Balloon 244 is watched by the amazed passengers for St Annes standing at the bus stop. If only Blackpool was now operating a tram service to St Annes Square, passengers would still be able to see comfortable trams turning the corner from Lytham Road - alas, never since 1937. Of course in 1959 this was a unique sight - hence the tram being pursued by two boys on their bikes! *Author*

Left Showing SQUIRES GATE & AIRPORT on its indicator, Balloon 257 arrives at the terminus from the Cabin and the conductor is about to turn the trolley. Passengers are standing at the stop about to board, while in the distance a single-deck railcoach approaches from Bispham, alternating with the double-deckers. The northbound tram track rounding the corner in the foreground is used by the Circular trams, while the St Annes-bound track is disappearing under the road surface. In June 1959 this is an exclusive residential area. *Author*

Below Squires Gate in the autumn of 1961, with only a few weeks left, and here two railcoaches, 282 and 214, pass near the terminus. Behind the trams can be seen the aircraft hangar of the Airport, which was opened in June 1931 and used during the war as a military airfield by RAF Coastal Command. During the Fifties the wartime aircraft factory was re-opened to assemble the Hawker Hunter jet-fighters, and flight services were operated by BIA to London, Belfast, Dublin and the Isle of Man. SQUIRES GATE & AIRPORT was thus the distinctive destination for the trams on this route. *Author*

BLACKPOOL TRAMS 1950-1966

Lytham Road

Here is a striking view of two railcoaches passing each other at Roseacre, showing tree-lined Lytham Road and the Tower in the distance. There was a tram every ten minutes to the Cabin and every ten minutes to Bispham, providing a five-minute headway to-and-from Squires Gate. In the early and late season railcoaches operated on the route, but in the busy height of the season six double-deckers are operated by Rigby Road depot on the Cabin route alternating with Bispham depot's seven single-deckers. Along the Promenade there were separate shelters for the Squires Gate service cars, provided with a notice 'Watson Road for Pleasure Beach'. Holidaymakers could therefore approach the Pleasure Beach via the Lytham Road route and walk down Watson Road; sometimes they showed alarm when the tram turned off the Promenade at Manchester Square, and left the tram to the local residents! *A. D. Packer collection*

At Skew Bridge the trams crossed the railway line, giving the passengers a view of South Station with its long platforms serving the junction with the 'fast line' from Kirkham. In the right distance can be seen the floodlights of Blackpool Football Club in Bloomfield Road. The tram is approaching an elegant pair of traction-poles surmounted by spiked finials and each carrying a pair of lights. *Author*

A line of passengers waits at the tram-stop for Squires Gate, but they are disappointed when the approaching tram turns off into Station Road, bound for South Pier! This was the only street route on the Blackpool system with common working between two routes; the Marton trams joined Lytham Road at Royal Oak and left it after one stop, at the Grand Hotel. On this quiet Sunday in Lytham Road in the autumn of 1961, the elegant Rover follows the tram lines over Skew Bridge - notice the boy on his delivery bike! *Author*

BLACKPOOL TRAMS 1950-1966

A Marton tram, 20, returning from South Pier rounds the sharp curve from Station Road into Lytham Road, pursued by a Vauxhall Victor with a poodle in the rear window! If you look closely at the roof of the shop above the tram, you may see old white lettering reading 'LYTHAM TRAMS HERE'. For many years this was the terminus of trams to Lytham St Annes via Squires Gate, after which the route crossed the municipal border. To the right of the tram, the Grand Motors building was originally the site of South Station. The long queue of passengers is looking down Lytham Road for the next tram to Squires Gate. *Author*

This tram is destined for Bispham, and the passengers are keen for its arrival from Squires Gate. This was of course the most direct route to Talbot Square, rather than travelling via Marton. Since the traffic is light it is safe for the passengers to board the tram in the road. Many of the houses in this section of Lytham Road have become business premises - shops and banks - in September 1961. *Author*

Here is a busy view on 19 September 1959 seen from the balcony of Standard 40, which is turning left from Waterloo Road into Lytham Road at Royal Oak junction. The time by the Transport clock is 6.38, which indicates that it is time for the 'specials' to travel to the Tower for the Illuminations Tour. Railcoach 267 is destined for 'CABIN', followed by Standard 41 for Central Station, and sandwiched between them is a Morris Commercial van. Behind 41 can be seen the striking building of the Lido, for 'Swimming' and 'Dancing'; owned by the Corporation, it was used by the local residents generally. *Author*

BLACKPOOL TRAMS 1950-1966

At Royal Oak junction the largely empty tram 41 passes the old Dog and Partridge Hotel on the corner of Waterloo Road. Behind it there is a coach park, where the vehicles stood for the day, and from where Standerwick Coaches operated daily trips to a variety of destinations including the Lake District. Overlooking the hotel is a large wall of adverts to catch the eye, including 'Let Capstan take the strain', 'Wm Younger's Beer', and Kodak Film to record it all! A taxi passes the tram, followed by Vauxhall Velox and MG Magnette saloons. The overhead wire looks very shaky on the curve. *Author*

On 24 May 1959 a visitor to Lytham Road is the strange tram Pantograph 175 from the Tramroad route to Fleetwood, giving enthusiasts a tour of the tramway system. It is certain that it has attracted the curiosity of the little boy with his Mum, seeing this large green monster - a rarity! What does the driver of the following Jaguar think? This is the only curve on Lytham Road, just before Bloomfield Road Football Ground, and is a busy shopping centre, showing a ladies' millinery shop next to Bob Dugdale's cafe advertising Holland's Pies & Puddings. *A. D. Packer collection*

A busy scene on Lytham Road in September 1961, as Brush railcar 301 approaches with its more modern single indicator-box showing BISPHAM via PROMENADE. In addition to all the shops with their sun-blinds, at the junction of Nelson Road on the right is the famous sports store of Stan Mortensen, Blackpool and England footballer. Many cars are parked here, largely for their owner's shopping, and include a Ford Prefect on the right, a Zephyr beside the tram and an Anglia on the left. *Author*

The Corner Cafe stands at the junction of Hopton Road and overlooks the junction of the tram track with the approach line to Rigby Road Depot and the Coliseum Coach Station. In the road can be seen clear marks of a derailed tram's wheels on the depot's curve. During the Illuminations the trams carry a string of coloured bulbs on their trolley tower, making their mobile contribution to the event. *Author*

A view of Manchester Square, where the Squires Gate route rejoined the Promenade reservation at the end of Lytham Road; the Coronation car is, however, leaving the depot and has never been down the Lytham Road route. This may be because of its 50-foot length, which would 'ground' its platform on Skew Bridge, leaving it stranded at the summit. This is a peaceful scene in 1955, with waiting boats along the shore and the Central Pier with its fishing jetty. The approaching green-liveried Balloon will be turning left here for Squires Gate. *Author's collection*

This is the only stretch of street route - Princess Parade - for the trams on the Promenade route, behind the Metropole Hotel. The first Blackpool tram track was laid here in 1885, using the conduit system. The scene reminds us of a city tramway, with traditional Standard tram 160 of 1927 approaching, followed by a railcoach. Along the Metropole Building is a row of shops, including the famous 'The Golden Age' furniture store, opposite the Princess cinema. Here trams are proceeding southwards on the wrong side of the road, and motorists should pass on the left - unless the one here is turning right into Springfield Road! *Author*

TALBOT SQUARE, ROYAL OAK AND SOUTH PIER VIA MARTON

AT THE beginning of the 20th century the Promenade trams had become successful, profitable and extensive between The Gynn and South Shore. Therefore Blackpool Council decided to create a new four-mile tramway throughout the urban area, away from the Promenade and providing a largely undeveloped rural area with public transport. The route was planned commencing in Talbot Square before the Town Hall, and would travel to Marton via Clifton Street, Abingdon Street, Church Street and Whitegate Drive.

Just before Preston Old Road on Whitegate Drive, with the Saddle Inn at the corner, the imposing Marton tram depot was constructed. It housed *circa* 48 trams on eight tracks, each with inspection pits and a large pair of green wooden doors. Surmounting the doors, upon twin gable-ends painted cream, was the shapely carved Municipal coat-of-arms. Passing the depot and reaching Oxford Square, the trams reached their greatest distance from the seafront, and turned west along Waterloo Road towards South Shore. At the Waterloo Hotel the trams turned right

towards Central Station. Here the new tramway was initially laid through open fields until it reached streets at Revoe Library; subsequently Central Drive was constructed round the new tram track, and housing development was stimulated by the new tram service. A link-line to the Royal Oak on Lytham Road was built in 1902.

Talbot Square is the centre of Blackpool, dominated by the handsome Town Hall, finished in 1900 and surmounted by an elegant spire complete with 'Golden Hind' weather vane. The Clifton Hotel on the right, rebuilt in 1866, forms a fine facade to the Marton tram terminus in the centre of the Square. This delightful scene from the Fifties shows the modern streamlined trams travelling along distant Clifton Street to terminate adjacent to the ornamental shelter. On the left-hand side - until 1936 the terminus of the Layton trams - is a modern bus built by Burlinghams of Blackpool, on route 22 to Halfway House. In the background, at the end of Clifton Street, is the splendid GPO building of 1903 in Abingdon Street, which is now listed by the Civic Trust. In the foreground can be seen the facilities of the centre island, some underground, including a barber with his striped signs. A tall Belisha beacon on the centre island of the road helps some pedestrians to cross towards the Promenade and North Pier. *Valentine & Sons, Dundee*

The opening of the Marton route in May 1901 was marked by some problems with the laying of the new tram track, which had wide grooves. This affected the riding quality of the new four-wheel open-toppers, which had difficulty getting into the depot until the curved-fan was relaid by November. The inaugural journey along Church Street with a civic party was delayed by cyclists objecting to the danger of the street tram track. However, the tram service was intended essentially for the benefit of tram passengers.

In the succeeding year, 1902, a short mile-long tram route was made from Talbot Square to Layton Cemetery via Talbot Road and the Abattoir. This route opened with trams having a 1st-class lower saloon and a 2nd-class open top deck, but it did not survive longer than 34 years because it was not extended to serve the housing development at Hoo Hill near Layton Station. Buses commenced serving that area from 1925, and competed with the trams from the Town Hall to the Cemetery along Talbot Road.

The new Marton Depot housed all the trams for the town routes, and additionally accommodated 'toast-racks' for the Circular Tour from 1911, together with the Dreadnoughts for the Promenade route. During the winter 20 or 30 trams were used for football specials, travelling in convoys along Central Drive to Bloomfield Road football ground. This was very useful until the closure of the Central Drive line in 1936, after which the Marton service operated a three-minute headway to Royal Oak, in the summer season extending to South Pier via Lytham Road and Station Road every nine minutes.

During the Thirties there was a plan to modernise the

Talbot Square to Church Street

Passengers beside the portico of the shelter await the arrival of the next Marton tram, which is adjacent to the St Annes bus. Behind them stands Yates's Wine Lodge, which also includes the Tivoli Cinema. Originally opened in 1868 as the Assembly Rooms, with restaurant, wine lodge and billiards, as the Theatre Royal it became one of the first theatres in Blackpool. Looking up Talbot Road to the left, we can see the large tiled building of the Bus Station and Car Park, which was opened in 1938 and remains today in disguise. As the service tram approaches its terminus, the driver has already turned its indicators to ROYAL OAK VIA MARTON, ready to return on time. *Author*

The same view in 1994 shows that Yates's Wine Lodge was restored in that year, celebrating its centenary in that role. The small bus occupies the approximate location of the tram, while the double-decker heads for the Bus Station. On the left of Talbot Road the tower of the Sacred Heart RC church of 1857 is under restoration. *Author*

tramway system and develop the bus route network, including the converted Layton and Central Drive lines. However, while modern streamlined trams were introduced to all the Promenade and Fleetwood routes, Marton continued with its traditional double-deck Standards throughout the war.

The Marton route thus survived into the post-war years as something of an anachronism, the duration of the Second World War preventing the relaying of the track and the introduction of modern trams. By 1945 there was no immediate decision by the Council to modernise the town tram route, and consideration was given to rival costs of buses, trolleybuses and trams. Manager Walter Luff, however, arranged a demonstration in April 1946 by a tram fitted with silent wheels and modern control equipment. The press described the riding over the disintegrating Marton track as 'sensational', and stated that 'its retention would be in line with modern ideas'. In January 1947 the Council decided to relay the Marton route to secure its future, and to introduce 1939 sun-saloon trams refitted with new equipment and resilient-wheeled bogies. By 1948 the first modern tram, No 10, went into service, and by January 1952 the entire

urban service was maintained by speedy and efficient trams.

For ten years the modern Marton service was provided by very comfortable, smooth-riding and rapidly accelerating trams, and was the finest tram service in post-war Britain. The local people liked the fast and efficient trams, and were proud of their independent tram route. During the summer season holidaymakers travelled to Stanley Park by tram, from Talbot Square or South Pier. However, during the Fifties, as the years went by, car ownership increased, affecting traffic on the tram route and reducing the passengers. In cities such as Liverpool, Leeds, Sheffield and Glasgow the trams were being replaced by buses, concluding in 1962.

In 1960 Blackpool's Council made the decision that they could not afford the renewal of the deteriorating Lytham Road route, and would close it at the end of the 1961 season. A year later, the isolated Marton route would also close, to the dismay - and petition - of the residents. On 28 October 1962 Marton's last tram procession from Talbot Square signalled the finale of British street tramways. A large crowd gathered at Marton Depot to witness their departure, and MARTON became NOTRAM!

Looking now towards the seafront in 1962 we see the next tram for Royal Oak standing with its trolley turned for departure, but its driver not yet in the cab. This is the time of the Illuminations, and you can see the strings of lights decorating the shelter as well as the tram. At the North Pier is Bernard Delfont's 'Show of Stars', and Charlie Parsons. If you wanted to stroll along the North Pier, opened in 1863, it would cost you sixpence. To the right of tram 14 is the Bundy time-clock with which the conductor punches his waybill with the departure time. *Author*

A wet evening in 1961 reflects the headlamps of the two Marton trams standing side-by-side in Talbot Square, as well as the lights of the Illuminations. The tram nearest to the Clifton has turned its trolley and is ready to go, while the driver of the other uses the trolley pole to reverse it. 'All traffic turn right' says the large sign, indicating that this is a weekend when Promenade traffic runs from south to north to view the Lights. *R. P. Fergusson*

Above The curve from Clifton Street into Abingdon Street was the sharpest on the tramway system, hence the 'No parking, Keep clear' painted on the road here. This striking view of the shopping street shows the Marton tram stretched across the curve and swung out at the back. The overhead is shaped by the span wires attached to rosettes on the front of the GPO on the right, some of which can be seen to this day. Looking along Abingdon Street can be seen a wide variety of shops, including Dewhurts butchers, a Stylo shoe shop and Batesons toy shop. Beyond Talbot Road in the distance can be seen the tower of Christ Church (1866), and beyond it the impressive building of Blackpool Public Library and Grundy Art Gallery, opened in 1911, can be glimpsed. Cars are parked in Abingdon Street before the days of double yellow lines, while the tram is passed by a cement lorry and a Morris Oxford, followed by a Wolseley. *W. R. Buckley*

Left Seen now from street level, having swung round the curve into Clifton Street this tram narrowly misses the parked Triumph Herald with its centre doors! Behind, on the corner, is H. Hunter's men's shop, which was well known for its mounted horse emblem. The pedestrian looks for the tram to move out of his way to cross the road. The conductor has turned the rear indicators ready for when the tram reverses in Talbot Square. *Author*

'ALL CARS STOP HERE' in Abingdon Street, outside the Market, Sally Mae Frocks and opposite the new Timothy Whites chemist shop. The traffic is halted by the passengers boarding the tram, unable to overtake on the inside because of the parked van. Yorkshire Bank is on the corner of Church Street, into which the tram track swings in the foreground. Trams dominate the scene in the centre of the road, and alternate street lights support the overhead. *Author*

The tram swings round the corner into Church Street, pursued by a taxi. The names of two famous shops are well remembered: Burton's confectioners and cafe next to Sweet & Clarke, gloves and hosiery for ladies. The latter was a famous traditional store with attended counters and where the cash received from customers was sent to the cashier in a sealed tin, travelling on a network of overhead wires. A tram was derailed on this curve in 1947 and ran into Sweet & Clarke's shop, causing damage. The track was subsequently relaid, and the old Standard double-deckers were replaced by streamlined trams. *Author*

Travelling down Church Street towards Abingdon Street a service tram passes between St John's parish church and the Opera House towards Paige's shoe shop. While the trams did not stop here, there was a bus shelter outside the church, which still remains today. In the street the trams kept the cars in line, parked like the Austin van on the left or passing like the Ford Anglia. *Author*

Looking up Church Street one sees a vintage tram passing the Hippodrome Theatre on the left, which opened in 1895 as The Empire. Every season the Hippodrome featured a Seasonal Show, which here in 1958 features Winifred Atwell at the piano, Michael Holliday. and the Nit-Wits in 'Light up the Town'. The auditorium was so high that, to reduce it, drapes were hung to form an artificial ceiling. The stage was also very high, and in one show called 'Up The Pole', starring Jewell and Warris, it housed a coconut grove, and coconuts were thrown from a great height! Behind tram 41 can be seen the marble dome of the Regent Cinema at the corner of Regent Road, still there today but used for bingo. *John Fozard collection*

By the time of this 1962 view the Hippodrome was being rebuilt by ABC as a modern luxury theatre seating 1,800. In its last season the Marton tram passes the restructured frontage, contrasting with the tower of St John's church, seen behind. On the official notice it is declared that the new theatre will include the latest technique in presenting stage shows and all forms of film including Cinerama and Cinemascope. So this would be a new cinema for the town throughout the year, with a live show for the Summer Season. What a shame that passengers won't be able to go by tram in 1963! *Author*

Further along Church Street, at Raikes Parade, vintage Standard tram 48 seems to be destined for Layton, but the route was converted to buses in 1936. However, 48 is at home on the Marton route on its last day of tram service, and is pursued by a bus on route 15A. Being a Sunday the shops are closed; likewise Blackpool Grammar School on the right. In the distance can be seen 'Kirby's for Cars' garage and filling station, still there today. The sun shines after a shower, and the handsome tram is reflected in the glossy road. Since 1964 Standard 48 has been at Glenwood Trolley Park in Oregon, USA. *Author*

Devonshire Square

On a spring day - 17 March 1961 - Marton Vambac 21 passes Whitesides on the corner of Cambridge Road, while ladies admire the knitwear in the window. Devonshire Square is the next stop, where the No 3 public house of 1872 can be seen facing Church Street. Here the tram will swing to the right, in front of the charming shelter where the passengers are waiting. The sunshine of the afternoon reflects in the tram's curved window and stainless steel fender, illuminating the attractive scene. *Author*

Well, today the trams are no longer sweeping round the corner here into Devonshire Square, and the shelter on the island has gone. However, all the buildings are still here: the No 3 pub, Midland Bank and the popular chip shop, together with the trees. The Marton route is now operated by the yellow and black 'Handy Buses' of Blackpool Transport - who still operate trams on the Promenade. *Author*

From the tram window the passenger can enjoy the sights along the route, and here at Devonshire Square we draw to a halt at the tram stop. However, in the foreground is a wrapped bus-stop sign ready for buses on the following day, for 28 October 1962 is the last day for a ride on a Marton tram. The pedestrian crossing leads to Fell's - a popular chip shop to this day - a sweet and cigarette shop, and the Midland Bank. Behind the shelter is the well-known No 3 public house. *Author*

ALL CARS STOP HERE at Devonshire Square, where, at the curve into Whitegate Drive, we get a better view of the attractive shelter with facilities for tram passengers and a clock tower surmounted by a weather vane. There is a bench to rest while waiting for the next tram, and a Belisha beacon for the pedestrians crossing to the shops. Railcoach 200 swings into the curve on 20 September 1962, and is very close to the waiting passengers - for safety. *Author*

Destined for SOUTH PIER & BATH, traditional double-decker 147 leaves Devonshire Square along Whitegate Drive in 1954. While the older passengers were happy to sit in the lower saloon, the youngsters always loved going upstairs where they got a good view of the territory! This splendid view gives a perspective on the road junction of the Square. The road sign on the left indicates a left turn to the Town Centre, right to Poulton-le-Fylde and straight ahead for Fleetwood. *Geoff Hyde*

Whitegate Drive

A scene from the Sixties as a young lady in a short skirt boards the tram at a 'Tram Stop, Temporary' just before the traffic lights at Hornby Road in Whitegate Drive. This was a popular stop for nearby Stanley Park, which opened in 1926 and includes a boating lake, beautiful gardens and sports grounds. Here the traffic waits until the nearside lane is clear for the cars to overtake the tram on the inside. Pads for the traffic lights can be seen beside and within the tram track, but the tram signals by its trolley through an 'ear' in the overhead line. Given a green light the modern tram can rapidly accelerate and leave motor vehicles standing! *Author*

A short-working at Palatine Road on 29 April 1962, and the driver runs round tram 11 with its trolley, ready to return to Royal Oak. Although Marton Vambac 15 looks as though it is heading for town, it could be reversing if the roads are closed in the Town Centre because of a Sunday parade! During the week this was a busy tram stop serving the shopping area and also the Palatine Road Secondary School, with hundreds of pupils. There were school specials using double-decker trams on the Marton route before 9 am and at 4 pm, and they stopped here. *Author*

Left On a fine evening in 1962, with the sun reflecting in the chrome frame of the windscreen, the conductor stands in the open doorway getting a suntan. The road is deserted, leaving the tram dominant. Bound for Royal Oak on route 13, the tram is passing the Health Centre, and behind can be seen the First Church of Christ the Scientist. Today there are some flats here, but Whitegate Drive is still very suburban with its hedges and trees - and today is very busy with traffic! *Colin Macleod*

Below Beechfield Avenue, with Elmslie Girls School located behind double-decker tram 48, is the pleasant location of this photograph taken on Sunday 28 October 1962. With the tyre marks showing in the rain on the nearside, the Ford Zodiac overtakes correctly. However, look out for the 'Tram Pinch' sign on the corner to warn that the tram lines swing inwards. The circular tram stop signs, such as that on the right, are mounted on a trolley pole that is painted with a red band and white hoops. However, note also the little bus-stop sign beyond it, discreetly covered with paper - until tomorrow! *Author*

BLACKPOOL TRAMS 1950-1966

Marton

At Marton Whitegate Drive widens for the forecourt of Marton Depot, which is flanked by the shopping centre. The eight tracks left the depot and curved to join a siding parallel to the service track, its pointwork set in cobbles. The 12 service trams left the west side of the depot first thing in the morning, followed by double-deckers as school specials. Once the rush-hour was over, trams emerged from the east side of the depot as 'specials' on the Promenade. Standard 160 is leaving, and the shed man is swinging its trolley pole while the other carries a point-iron in his hand to move the points during shunting. The tram stands outside a newsagent, which is still there to this day - unlike the tram depot! *R. P. Fergusson*

On a sunny day in 1960 the empty Boat tram is setting off for the Promenade, while the service tram is halted at the stop. The 12 Boat trams were housed at Marton Depot, and were frequently used for the Circular Tour. The depot doors are swung open and some staff cars are parked in front of the office where the depot Inspector presides over the cashier, into whose office the conductors pay their collected fares and have a break in the crew room. A tall pole in the centre of the forecourt carries a clock, floodlights and the overhead feeder line. This is certainly a centre of action! *R. P. Fergusson*

Today the road is still very wide at this point, and the gap between the shops is filled by a BP service station. If you look behind it you will see the rear section of the tram depot, now used as an industrial premises. The newsagents is neighboured by the Saddle Chippy, a popular venue together with the famous Saddle Inn of 1776 with its traditional style and real ale. *Author*

Left Travelling on the wrong side of the road, Standard 160 is about to cross over opposite the tram shelter, while the conductor rides on the step holding the trolley pole. An Austin A40 overtakes, while an older Austin is parked outside the shops, including a gents hairdresser, Susi for ladies and a pet shop. Today the scene is full of shops and traffic, but without the trams. *R. P. Fergusson*

Below left Trams pass Marton's parish church of St Paul in Whitegate Drive on a spring day in 1962, and a lady steps into the road at the tram stop. Fortunately the traffic was quiet in those days and passengers could step into the road safely. The school sign showing children skipping into the road indicates the location of Baines Endowed School, founded in 1717. Through the winter trees can be seen the houses facing on to Preston Old Road and the gable end of the 1776 Saddle Inn. The tram on the left, bound for Talbot Square, approaches Marton shopping centre and Depot, where the crew will change for their break in the crew room. *Author*

Below When the trams reached Oxford Square they were at the furthest point to the east of the Promenade tramway, and the route curved back towards the coast again, at South Pier. Preston New Road is divided by an island; note the railings that protect the steps down to the air-raid shelter built during the Second World War. The Scammell three-wheeler with trailer, carrying packing cases for British Railways, waits for the tram to pass. The large houses on the main road indicate a quality residential area; in front of the first is a neat bus shelter and telephone kiosk. *Evening Gazette, Blackpool*

Waterloo Road

Marton service cars pass on the crossover at Oxford Square at the top of Waterloo Road in front of the passenger shelter surmounted by a clock tower. Behind the tram's trolley towers can be seen the local Blackpool Co-operative store. A very handsome Riley car approaches from Preston New Road and will overtake the tram on the inside. One of the adverts on the shelter shows the new Coastal Tour of 1958, by twin trailer trams. *David Packer collection*

Here in Waterloo Road the tram leaves the Oxford Square shelter behind and heads for the Royal Oak terminus, passing the local shops. Some shoppers have arrived in cars, notably Morris Minors on each side. The modernised cottages in Vicarage Lane on the right are covered with pebbledash, adding an air of smartness. *Author*

At the Rectory Road stop the tram sweeps to a halt as the passengers step into the road and one shares the camera! The uniformed conductor appears in the doorway and will raise his arms to halt any following traffic. Being an autumn Sunday in 1962 the trees are bare, the traffic is light and the sunshine is reflected in the windscreen. Construction of flats can be seen further down Waterloo Road - a new age. *Author*

Having swung round Spen Corner, the junction of Waterloo Road with Ansdell Road, Hawes Side Lane and Marton Drive, the tram is bound for South Pier on a warm 12 September 1959. The windscreens are wide open for the driver to enjoy sunbathing in uniform! A passenger waits at the tram stop outside Waterloo Road Primary School, behind the neat railings and row of trees that shade the playground. Note the heavy street lights and newly suspended overhead line from the span wire. This could cope with pantographs, if fitted. *Author*

Blackpool South Station stands at the summit of the road over the railway lines that the tram now climbs, approaching the Royal Oak terminus. Notice that the driver on route 19 has already changed his indicators to Talbot Square ready for the return journey. Looking down the road a long procession of vehicles can be seen, while the tram has gained a head start by its rapid acceleration. Behind the fence on the left, being passed by the Austin Cambridge, are the carriage sidings where were stored many excursion trains from Central Station. Today a single railway line terminates at South Station and the railway sidings have become a car park on a vast scale! *Author*

BLACKPOOL TRAMS 1950-1966

Royal Oak

During the winter Marton trams terminated here at Royal Oak on Lytham Road, and reversed in the centre of the road outside the entrance to the Palladium Cinema. The shopping centre continues along Waterloo Road, across Lytham Road, towards the seafront. Above the tram can be seen an advert for Capstan and the roof of the vintage Dog & Partridge Hotel (see page 15). In the Fifties the streamlined trams were painted in this livery, with green 'Vs' at each end and 'sweeps' on each side. This was a reversal of the wartime green livery. *David Packer collection*

A busy scene at Royal Oak terminus on 23 May 1959, with cyclists signalling to turn right, while the trams are stationary. Railcoach 266 is destined for Talbot Square via Marton, while Balloon 244 - in vintage livery - has just arrived from Squires Gate on tour. Two ladies walk from the kerbside tram stop behind the Balloon to board the service car. When its driver hears the signal bell, the tram will climb the bridge, its trolley having reversed automatically - very practical in traffic! The first stop will be Blackpool South Station. *Author*

Above During the summer season every third Marton tram turned into Lytham Road in front of Royal Oak Hotel, bound for South Pier. This was useful for passengers heading for the South Shore - the Open Air Baths or the Pleasure Beach. *Author*

Left In 1994 there are no trams at Royal Oak, but alternatively you could use a vintage landau such as the one seen here following the former tram route by turning right into Waterloo Road. Today there are traffic lights; Barclays Bank survives, as does the Royal Oak pub; while the Palladium is now for bingo. *Author*

BLACKPOOL TRAMS 1950-1966

Station Road, seen during the summer season with a Marton tram, looks very clean and tidy with terraces of hotels and shops. The tram is passing the crossing of Bond Street, which continues behind the Pleasure Beach and where was situated the sub-station that supplied South Shore trams with power. Along each side of the road are parked cars and vans, clear of the track, including contrasting Vauxhall, Ford Anglia and Bentley. Happily the tram has a non-stop journey to South Pier. *Author*

The driver of this tram on route 40 looks happy as he approaches the terminus at South Pier, with his windscreen open and his indicators changed ready for return. Notice that the motorcyclist waits for the tram to pass before he sets off . . . without a crash helmet in 1961! Visitors sit in the garden of one of the hotels, enjoying the sunshine during the autumn Illuminations - hence the lights on the trolley tower of the tram. *Author*

The terminus of the inland Marton route was opposite South Pier, being extended along Station Road during the Summer Season. Having a swivel-head on its trolley, railcoach 265 reaches out to the overhead above the curve, where the line is linked with the Promenade route. This August 1958 scene shows holidaymakers going back to their hotels for tea, or the cafe seen here with fish and chips at 1s 9d. The ladies look attractive in their summer frocks, but two of the young men are wearing 'cowboy' stetsons. The modern Burlingham centre-entrance bus 257 was one of a fleet 100 strong - unique to Blackpool during the Fifties. Loading on route 10, it will be destined for Midgeland Road via Royal Oak. *Author*

NORTH STATION AND FLEETWOOD

THE Blackpool & Fleetwood tram service is still running to this day, an amalgamation between the Promenade tramway of 1885 and the inter-urban line from Gynn Square to Fleetwood Ferry. The tramroad was founded by an independent company in 1897, having been surveyed along the coast by John Cameron, appointed as Manager from the Manx Northern Railway. The tramroad was recognised by the House of Lords as a railway, and therefore only paid a quarter of its rates to Fleetwood, Cleveleys and Bispham with Norbreck UDCs, through which it ran. Blackpool Corporation granted access to the company's trams with running powers from the boundary at Cliffs to Talbot Road station via the 'backroad' route. This accorded it a second-class status relative to their new proposed Promenade line from Cocker Street to The Gynn.

When the first tram made an experimental run to Fleetwood on 1 July 1898 'an exhilarating ride' was enjoyed by the official Municipal and Company passengers on open crossbench car 4: 'The feeling was grand'. When it arrived in Fleetwood, crowds of flag-waving children and enthusiastic locals greeted it in Lord Street, marking the beginning of a new age of 'The New Electric Car'.

From the beginning 'One of the Joys of Life is a ride on the Blackpool & Fleetwood Cars', and it became most successful as transport for the local community and holidaymakers alike. However, when the lease of the Blackpool track to the company terminated in 1919, a decision was made to sell the Tramroad to the Corporation, with effect from 1 January 1920. Hence it became an integrated part of the Blackpool Corporation Tramway, and its trams were repainted in the Municipal red and white livery. The tram tracks were connected at Gynn Square, and eventually the Promenade trams operated to Bispham, and the Squires Gate service to Cabin in

In 1898 the Tramroad terminated immediately in front of Talbot Road station, as it was originally known under Lancashire & Yorkshire Railway ownership when it opened in 1846; later it became known as Blackpool North. This enabled tram passengers to disembark outside the main entrance and enter the station directly on a Saturday, carrying their luggage. During the working week the early morning trams were full of travellers by railway to Manchester - and other Lancashire towns - on business. The North Station building, which was re-designed in this style in 1896, was admired for its handsome clock tower and the sheltering veranda. Behind the Fleetwood tram - Pantograph car 172 - can be seen the Talbot Hotel public house, which had a famous bowling green. Looking along Caunce Street the tall roof of the Hippodrome can be seen in Church Street. The tram is flanked by cars heading for Talbot Road, and the West Yorkshire Bristol express bus on route J1 is bound for Fleetwood from Leeds. Thus the terminus was a busy place, full of passengers and traffic.
Author

1924. The Fleetwood service continued with the single-deck tramroad cars on a regular ten-minute headway from North Station, and it was known as No 1.

In that era it is interesting to note that the route at Rossall School was re-aligned to its present location, avoiding the sharp curve and the school gates. In 1924 the terminal loop to Fleetwood Ferry was constructed, taking the trams to the Promenade and past Pharos Lighthouse - of lasting fame to this day! Additionally, in 1927 sidings were built at Thornton Gate, and freight trains of coal wagons were drawn by an electric locomotive from a connection with the railway behind Copse Road Depot. Thus coal was delivered to Cleveleys by a tramway train - unique!

Development of the property along the Tramroad took place during the Twenties and Thirties, and the seafront carriageway was built north of Norbreck to Anchorsholme alongside the Tramroad. New trams were introduced in two generations, first the Pullmans in 1928, which were in the inter-urban tradition of the USA. However, they were fitted with a pantograph rather than the familiar trolley, which gave them their popular name.

Then in the Thirties came the Tramway Revolution, under the new Manager Walter Luff, when streamlined rail-coaches were introduced to the Fleetwood route. It was established that the journey, 8.16 miles from North Station, could be done with stops in 30 minutes. This was very comfortable for the passengers, and the railcoaches competed with motorcoaches that ran excursions to Fleetwood on Market Day. In 1940, during the Second World War, the former Company Depot at Bispham was re-opened for trams on route 1. Its staff maintained the tradition of 'the other firm' for the rest of its life, until 1963.

In post-war years, throughout the 'fifties, there were two tram services to Fleetwood from North Station and New South Promenade, with short workings to Cleveleys. This included a six-minute service, and only three minutes between Cleveleys and Gynn Square on the joint track. A great novelty occurred in 1958 when in July double-deckers were enabled to work for the first time to Fleetwood, the track having been fitted with check-rails for safety. On Market Day double-deckers ran as 'specials' from North Station along Dickson Road, carrying the many extra passengers. This increased capacity improved the popularity of Service 1 from the Town Centre to Fleetwood. Since the trams terminated at North Station, on Saturdays many visitors travelled there by tram from North Shore hotels with their luggage. When the traffic had become congested by 1960, the terminus was foreshortened in front of the Odeon and fitted with an automatic trolley reverser. This spared the conductors the job of swinging the tram's trolley in traffic.

However, the 'writing was on the wall' when street routes were closing in cities all over Britain; in Blackpool the Squires Gate and Marton tram routes, and finally that to North Station succumbed on 27 October 1963. The finale of the original 1898 Tramroad to Fleetwood took place when a procession left the terminus on the last night of the Lights. Bispham Depot closed, but the Fleetwood route survived with the Promenade route, where the trams were on reservations, except in Lord Street. This became the sole surviving street tramway in Britain, and will reach its century in 1998.

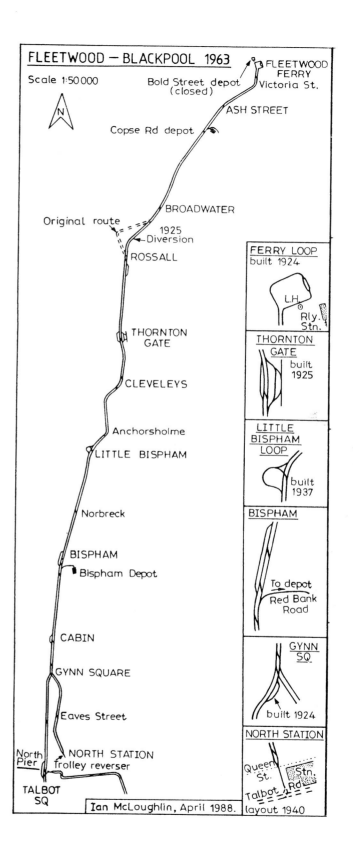

The Blackpool & Fleetwood Tramroad route in 1963.
Ian McLoughlin

North Station and Dickson Road

'ALL CARS STOP HERE' opposite the Odeon Cinema in Dickson Road, and 173 is fully loaded for Fleetwood while Brush railcar 291 proceeds towards the North Station terminus. The Bundy time-clock is mounted on the tram stop pole, ready for the conductor to clock the departure time and regulate the ten-minute service. Looking down Dickson Road, the Gwalia, on the corner of Springfield Road, leads the rows of boarding houses on each side of the road. The spires are the Unitarian Chapel of 1875 and the Methodist Church of 1913, the latter still in use today. There are many shops in this area, sheltered by their sun-blinds, while the cars are parked clear of the tram track. In the middle of the afternoon the traffic is represented by a solitary northbound Austin. *Author*

The end of the tram track was cut short to this point outside the Odeon Cinema by Easter 1961, to relieve traffic congestion before North Station. A trolley reverser was also fitted to allow easier reversal of the trams, without their conductors having to run round with the trolley pole amongst the traffic. The width of the road was such that it gave plenty of room for the trams to unload in the centre, leaving room for passing traffic and parked cars. There was also a busy bus stop in front of the Odeon parallel with the (safely) reversing tram. Here we see the rider of a scooter coming face to face with a Bentley pulling out from the kerb! The couple crossing the road are taking care, but also posing for the cameraman recording this scene. The Odeon, built in 1939, is a splendid building with its tiled facade of giant proportions, confirming that this was the largest cinema, with 3,000 seats! It is still there today, divided into three screens, but the trams departed in 1963 and are greatly missed. *Author*

The new loading barrier, with a lunchtime queue filing across the roadway to load upon tram 285. Note the words 'TRAM STOP' painted on the road, as a warning to motorists not to park. The duty Inspector is counting the number of passengers in the queue to fill this 48-seater, bound for Cleveleys. There are rows of shops and hotels as far as you can see, culminating in the Lansdowne Hotel, facing the Promenade. Naturally the loading tram halts the motorist in the Vauxhall, while an approaching Mini passes 'Honest Eds' across the road! *Author*

Double-decker trams appeared in Dickson Road for the first time in 1958, and dominate the scene in the middle of the traffic. In this view looking back towards North Station, the lorry seems to be carrying barrels under its tarpaulin, followed by a bus, heading for Victoria Hospital, leaving its Odeon stop. The approaching Mini car is dominated by the tall tram, which shows 'North Station Blackpool' on its indicator - the only destination that includes its home town! On the pole level with the tram there is a sign pointing to the Excursion platforms 7-16, which comprise today's North Station. Sadly the handsome station building has been replaced by a supermarket. The 'Private . . .' sign on the first building in Queens Street shows that hotels are present, near to the Public Library and Art Gallery. *Author*

The young pedestrians in the foreground stare, fascinated by the automatic reverser swinging the trolley of double-decker 247 out at right-angles to its body! This is the tea-time peak hour and the Balloon has been sent to relieve the queue at the terminus with a short working to Bispham . . . and the Airport? This will augment the five-minute service alternating to Cleveleys and Fleetwood. The shops at the side of the tall tram include a sweet shop with its Players Please advert, and Richmonds, selling exclusive attire. The frocks indicate that this is the Summer Season! *Author*

Tram 302 is outnumbered by three buses on its last day of service - 27 October 1963. However, this photograph was taken from a vintage Dreadnought tram at the terminus, hence the service tram is having its trolley turned with the bamboo pole held by a volunteer - Steve Palmer! In the street on the left, outside Wiseman's TV shop, a group of tram fans gathers to record the scene for the last time, one of whom sprinting at speed! Meanwhile the bus driver turns his back on the tram and heads for home. This is a memorable scene! *R. P. Fergusson*

BLACKPOOL TRAMS 1950-1966

The Carlton Hotel, built since Claremont Park was developed in 1863, is situated on the curve of Dickson Road, where the seafront is within sight. On the corner with Pleasant Street the Chemist & Optician is no doubt useful for both residents and holidaymakers. Brush car 295 swings round the curve in July 1963 and reflects the afternoon sun in its windscreen. The pedestrians are about to cross the road, perhaps returning to their hotels for tea. *Author*

A little further along Dickson Road we see holidaymakers who have been shopping, walking along the pavement behind the hotels and towards the rear of the large 1867 Imperial Hotel. Brush car 284 passes them on its way to Fleetwood, while the Mini is coming into town. The boarding house on the corner of Bute Avenue carries a sign for the famous Magnet Ales. This section of Dickson Road was widened in 1923 to enable the single tram track to be doubled, and facilitate the tram service. *Author*

'THORNTON GATE VIA CLEVELEYS' is the destination of this service car, which passes 'Geo. Whitehead - Decorator' and approaches Derby Road. Here, on the corner, stands the Elmhurst Private Hotel, with 'Excellent Food & Good Service', 'Moderate Charges' and a 'Car Park' for customers. In full view of the passengers are large advertisements: 'Real Dairy Cream', 'Mm! Pork for flavour!' and 'Player's new-size cigarette', the Richmonds. It is interesting to note that on 29 July 1963 284 has on its side panels the original chrome streamlining of 1937! *Author*

BLACKPOOL TRAMS 1950-1966

Gynn Square
and the Cabin

This 'Warley Road - Derby Baths' as Pantograph 169 approaches the stop, and passengers stand on the platform ready to get off. The trams always carried many local passengers along Dickson Road to Gynn Square, while holidaymakers rode to Fleetwood. These trams were the only ones to have trolley ropes, which were useful for the conductors and gave the trams a distinctive look. At each side are contrasting vehicles: bus 303, a new Burlingham Leyland PD2/21, on the 7A Bispham Circular, and a vintage car - a Singer Gazelle. An interesting scene from Easter 1960. *Author*

Brush car 295 climbs the gradient up from Gynn Square on 29 July 1963 passing a northbound tram descending to the stop. A cyclist is passed by the approaching tram together with parked cars, fronted by a Vauxhall saloon. The row of shops on the left with their sun-blinds represents the shopping area, facing some hotels on the opposite side. Looking across the Square in the distance, a railcoach is seen climbing Queens Drive reservation, giving its passengers a good view of the Irish Sea. *Author*

Looking down at Gynn Square from a little nearer, we see a busy scene with holidaymakers enjoying the sun near the shops and cafe. Railcoach 216, bound for North Station, loads at the tram-stop outside the Gynn Hotel, while a Hillman Minx and a Mini are parked on the hill. The previous service 1 tram has joined the Promenade track, and ascends the hill preceding the new all-cream trailer-tram as a special. The clock in the centre of the Square shows 12.25 for the benefit of the time-keeping tram drivers - and the public too. *Author*

Above This attractive scene looking up Dickson Road from Gynn Square shows the Gynn Hotel, which had been built by 1939 to replace the historic Gynn Inn demolished in August 1921. This stood next to the tram track in the middle of the Square, and was a famous landmark from the sea. Pantograph car 175 descends the hill and passes at speed through the Square, followed at a distance by cars. There is an attractive row of buildings up Dickson Road, including the modern Kays Carpet Shop and the Sunnyside Hotel. Passengers for North Station wait in front of the attractive cream-and-green shelter on the island, and are approached by an Austin A70 Hampshire car. *Author*

Below Brush car 301 has crossed Gynn Square and joins the Promenade tram reservation at this junction. The shelter is situated here for passengers to board the service 1 tram for Fleetwood; the feeder cable to this route's overhead is seen above the tram. Bound for 'THORNTON GATE CLEVELEYS', 301 alternates every ten minutes with Fleetwood service cars. The van of T. Walmsley & Son waits for the tram to cross its path, while an Austin Cambridge follows the white line up Queens Drive. While the trams and the traffic separate here, today the trams remain on their reservation and have not crossed Gynn Square since 1963. *Author*

To reach North Station, Pantograph 169 has turned off at the junction to cross Gynn Square and climb Dickson Road. This is a quiet day on the Easter Weekend of 1960, and the tram can proceed safely. At this junction there were automatic points, which the drivers operated by applying one notch of power to turn left. The points have just been reset through a skate in the overhead by 169's trolley, when has cleared the junction. The sunken gardens of the Twenties are situated across the Square on the left, giving the local hotels a pleasant view and location. *Author*

An attractive view of 168 approaching Gynn Square junction in 1960, with the Savoy Hotel looking impressive behind and flags flying by the Cliffs Hotel further down. The Brush car has just come from North Station and the people are strolling alongside the sunken gardens. The bracket arm on the pole next to the tram holds the skate that signals to the points for the tram to turn left into Gynn Square. Motorists have parked their cars along Queens Drive so that they can perhaps take a tram or enjoy a walk. If they walked up to the Cabin, they could use the lift down to the Boating Pool for a sail. *Author*

Outside Uncle Tom's Cabin and the New Cumberland Hotel, both trams have stopped for passengers and both are in the wartime style of livery. No 174 is on service 1 - note the number in the side-indicator-box of the saloon - followed by Balloon 237 for Pleasure Beach, while the new Coronation car on the extreme left is turning at the Cabin. This is the highest point of the coastal route, where one can get a splendid view across Morecambe Bay towards the Lake District, when the weather is clear. *Author*

Bispham

This is Red Bank Road, where the trams are the centre of attention en route to and from Bispham Depot, established by the Tramroad Company in 1898. Clearly Pantograph 172 has gained the attention of the passers-by as it travels up to Bispham Station with a blank indicator blind. Although passengers were not carried on this private route, tram crews going on duty at Bispham Top got a lift from the Depot. The Dominion Cinema provides another local attraction, showing *Pal Joey* this week. Today there are many shops and cafes here, but no trams or cinema. *R. P. Fergusson*

With a 'RESERVED' blind, 225 leaves Bispham Depot yard, and unusually starts its journey to Bispham Top filled with passengers. This is the last weekend of the tram depot - Saturday 26 October 1963 - when tramway enthusiasts enjoyed an unusual ride to North Station by Boat! Driver Tom Leeming - who started work in 1917 for the Tramroad Company - has become senior at Bispham Depot, and will drive the last tram. Naturally he remembers the Cameron family, who lived at 'Pooldhooie', the large house on the right, until 1920, and which is today the Conservative Club. The depot site is now occupied by a Sainsbury's supermarket, but the bowling green is still there, behind the wall. *Author*

BLACKPOOL TRAMS 1950-1966

Above Bound for North Station, 168 stops in front of the Norbreck Hydro Hotel, an imposing facade whose battlements along its roof have now renamed it 'Norbreck Castle'. During the Second World War civil servants evacuated from London worked in the building, and in 1943 staged a sit-down demonstration. 'Is your journey really necessary?' they chanted, as trams filled with holidaymakers failed to stop for the workers! All is well here in 1960, however, as the couple in the foreground begin a walk along the cliff top. *Author*

Below A delightful view from the open top deck of Dreadnought 59 at Little Bispham shows the passing trams on Service 1. Across the golf course - closed by 1960 - can be seen the houses of Cleveleys, the Queens Theatre on the seafront, and the chimney and cooling towers of Fleetwood Power Station. The tramroad curves right and drops in level from this high point, and has an emergency stop before the Anchorsholme crossing with Fleetwood Road. *R. P. Fergusson*

Cleveleys

Approaching Cleveleys Square on a double-decker tram provides a good view of the tramroad in the centre of the dual carriageway. First one sees the Orion, for bingo, formerly the Odeon Cinema, and along the crescent a row of shops and the post office. Today the scene looks much the same, except that the GPO is immediately adjacent to the Orion. Traditional Standard tram 147 is making its final journey to Fleetwood, before emigrating to USA in 1967. *Author*

Passing through the roundabout in Cleveleys Square, Pantograph 171 gives way to the Ribble saloon circling round it. Cleveleys developed as a shopping centre once the Tramroad brought passengers from Blackpool early in the century. Today it is very busy with residents and tourists arriving by tram, so that in the Summer Season a regular service, using Balloons, reverses here for the Pleasure Beach. *Author*

An elevated view of Cleveleys Square and the Pennines on the horizon, along with the ICI Works at Thornton. The railcoach in the wartime livery, which survived into the early Fifties, leaves its passenger shelter and passes through the island, which helps the traffic to circulate at the junction. The District Bank building looks impressive - one of four in the Square - which today is a branch of the National Westminster Bank. The Belisha beacons mark the crossing places for pedestrians, and today there are traffic lights, but no roundabout! *Author's collection*

The tram station with shelters enables passengers to board the trams safely, free from traffic, and Standard 147 passes railcoach 224 bound for the Tower. A couple with a child in a push-chair use the pedestrian crossing, halting the traffic and the following tram 158. Some of the old houses in Brighton Avenue have become shops - The Shoe Horn and a travel agent - still there today! The large house in York Avenue next to the tram lines was used by Duxbury's the solicitors, but today is demolished and replaced by an office. 'LRTL SPECIAL' fills 147's indicator, marking a historic last journey for its fans on 29 October 1966. *Author*

At the Cleveleys tram station, short-workings reversed for North Station and Starr Gate every ten minutes respectively. On the right a tram is arriving from Fleetwood followed by a Balloon, while passengers wait at a special shelter for service 1. Looking along Rossall Road we can see St Andrews parish church on the left, standing in its own grounds. An Austin passes the 'Trams for Fleetwood' tram shelter; today the traffic operates a one-way system round the tram station. *Author*

Thornton Gate and Rossall

Pantograph 173 is about to reverse at Thornton Gate; the conductor rides on the step of the platform, ready to turn the trolley with its rope. This is the site of the mineral sidings where coal was delivered by train until 1949, and in 1963 is used for the permanent way. This is an industrial estate between Cumberland Avenue and Westmoreland Avenue, where the semi-detached houses back on to the sidings. A loop line permits the Fleetwood trams to pass reversing short-workings such as 173. *Author*

Between Rossall and Broadwater, where the open landscape recalls the early days of the Tramroad before urban development took place, 175 is on a journey to North Station. On the left the farmer's field is faced by the houses of Melbourne Avenue; today it is the playing fields of Cardinal Allen High School. The right-hand side features King George V Playing Field and its changing rooms, still there today. The long grass includes tank traps, which date back to wartime days and were designed to resist invasion! *Author*

In August 1957 your author is waiting for a tram at Broadwater, where the A585 crosses the tramroad. Railcoach 218, in the attractive post-war livery, approaches the substantial shelter with waiting passengers. Local shops serve the Council estate, here featuring Broadwater Stores for groceries and 'Players Please'. The tram service is very useful for residents travelling to Fleetwood's main shopping centre, and on Market Days - Tuesday and Friday - a local service is operated between Broadwater and the Ferry. This is very useful, when full trams come from Blackpool in the morning and return in the afternoon full of visitors. *R. P. Fergusson*

Fleetwood

By December 1963 the busy tram service in Lord Street had become unique in Britain. Two railcoaches, 265 and 264, pass many shops, including optician Frank J. Fox, Henderson's men's clothes and, opposite, Woolworths. A lady with her shopping bag waits at the Ash Street tram stop, where there is a large shelter with a clock tower. The approaching tram is now bound for Central Station, since the North Station route had closed at the end of the Illuminations. Maybe she will have to change to a bus at Cleveleys, where trams terminated during that winter. *Author*

An elevated view of Lord Street from the Co-op building clock tower, looking back towards the location of the previous photograph and showing double-decker tram 260 heading for the Ferry and followed by a Ribble bus. On the corner of London Street is Williams Deacons Bank, adjacent to a row of shops with sun-blinds including Redman's Delicatessen, Hudson's for sweets and tobacco, a dispensing chemists and Reeco TV. The next row of shops starts with the famous Burtons Tailors on the corner, and includes the large Regent Cinema, which became the last in Fleetwood. Looking over the rooftops of the town centre, the trees of the Memorial Park can be seen, and, along Poulton Road, the distant tower of St Wulstan's RC church. At the end of Lord Street stands the National Provincial Bank and the dome roof of Elim Full Gospel Church, where the trams rejoined their reservation. The bell in the Co-op tower chimed the hour in clear tones, but sadly not today - a happy memory! *Author*

Above Having passed St Peter's parish church, the tram lines turn into North Albert Street, where two Coronation trams, 321 and 312, are passing near to the Market. Hardisty's butchers shop is on the corner of Adelaide Street, and between the trams can be seen the General Post Office of 1907. The parked cars on the left include a Vauxhall Victor and a Mark 1 Ford Cortina, and on the right a Singer Vogue and Ford Zephyr. The sun-blind of Parkinson's grocers shop has been familiar to local residents for many years. *Author*

Below 'Tram Pinch' indicates to traffic that the trams are about to swing across their path, as the single-line terminal loop turns into Bold Street. In 1961 the Brush car approaches the original terminal depot of 1899, which housed two trams - the last at night and the first in the morning. Over the doors can be seen the headstone for the Blackpool & Fleetwood Tramroad Company, and the adjacent office was for the inspector and crew. The building was demolished in 1973 and a block of flats stands in its place. However, the North Euston Hotel of 1841 is still present, along with the cafe and shops. *R. P. Fergusson*

Fleetwood terminus

The Pharos Lighthouse was built to guide shipping down the channel of the River Wyre - to be aligned with the Lower Lighthouse - and was situated unusually in the street. The trams passed the lighthouse for the first time in 1925, when the new terminal loop line was built. The passengers found the new Ferry terminus convenient to reach the Esplanade, ferry slipway and the Isle of Man steamer quay. The advertisement boards on the right conceal the bowling green, which could be seen from the top deck of a double-decker tram like Standard 40, seen on Sunday 24 May 1959. *Author*

A sight unique in Britain - trams passing a lighthouse in the street. Coronation 317 is in service to Starr Gate; swinging round the curve into Pharos Street, it seems to be waiting for a passenger! From this location near the station, the broadside view of the 50-foot tram, with its windows at three levels, well shows the handsome appearance. The seated passengers will be able to look up at the cream stem of the lighthouse surmounted by its red summit balcony. Over the front of the tram a sign points to the Lighthouse Garage, but Caton's Ices is closed today. The network of span wires curve the overhead into its location above the tram track, and ensure that the trolley stays in place. *Author*

At Fleetwood Ferry terminus the railcoach shares the scene with a ship sailing down the River Wyre into the harbour. A dredger keeps the Channel clear for the fleet of fishing vessels, the cargo ships and the Isle of Man steamer. The 63-mile sailings to Douglas commenced in 1842 and finished in 1961, when *Monas Queen* departed from the crumbling jetty. Ten years later, in 1971, *Monas Isle* returned, and the service continues to this day, in 1994 with the Sea Cat *Isle of Man*! The lifeboat house is seen at the corner. In an emergency the boat was launched down a slipway into the water; visitors toured the building to see the lifeboat and the record of rescues over many years since 1859. Although this looks to be a quiet day, the area is often crowded with visitors during the summer, many of whom have arrived by tram. *Author*

A busy scene in Clifton Street on 28 July 28 1962, as traditional Standard 48 returns to Marton Depot after a day on the Promenade, while the service car waits to enter Talbot Square terminus. Yates's Wine Lodge with it canopy contains the Tivoli Cinema, showing *Play It Cool*, a 1962 pop film starring Billy Fury, Helen Shapiro and Shane Fenton (better known today as Alvin Stardust), while the distant GPO facade provides an impressive scene for the Town Centre. *Author*

Central Promenade at 4.30 pm on a September afternoon in 1960, a colourful scene with Dreadnought 59 fully loaded for the Pleasure Beach, followed by service cars for Squires Gate and Starr Gate. Woolworths is flying the Union Jack, its architecture contrasting with the Palatine Hotel at the corner of Hounds Hill. Beneath the illummnated butterflies spanning the roadway traffic is busy, with a service bus trying to join the Promenade, while the landaus wait for customers to take a sunny ride. Holidaymakers stroll in the sunshine, well-dressed for the occasion - note the little boy with his cowboy hat! The colourful 'pagoda' is part of the Illuminations scene. *Author*

On the Marton route railcoach 207 performs 'Cars Stop By Request' at Beechfield Avenue on 6 July 1962, having just travelled from Royal Oak. This is a pleasant part of Whitegate Drive, with trees surrounding Elmslie Girls' School on the corner. A 'Tram Pinch' sign warns traffic of the cornering trams! *Author*

Outside the Odeon Cinema - at the terminus of the North Station route - railcoach 211 is reversing its trolley upon its return to Thornton Gate. The pre-war railcoach contrasts with the post-war bus on the 3 service to Newhouse Road, while the red lorry is delivering bags of coal in this 1963 scene. Dickson Road has a muster of shops, boarding houses and two churches. *Author*

A panoramic view of Lord Street, Fleetwood, from the Co-op building on a sunny day in June 1966. Coronation 308 - bound for Starr Gate - passes railcoach 264 at the corner of London Street, dominated by Williams Deacons Bank. A lady pushes her pram across the road after the tram has passed, proving that trams are always safely predictable. At this time Fleetwood remained the only shopping centre served by a tram service, but is now joined by Manchester and Sheffield in a new generation of trams. *Author*

'Fresh Fish Daily - Salmon a Speciality' at the Warley Road tram stop on Dickson Road in 1963, where the Brush car comes to a halt having just climbed the hill from Gynn Square. There is a Burlingham bus opposite. This was a popular location for passengers who may be shopping or visiting the famous Derby Baths here. The Accrington bricks give a lovely rouge tone to the area, and a large yellow arrow points down to the chemist shop. *Author*

THIS IS IT!
THE 75TH ANNIVERSARY, 1960

AS THE year 1960 dawned to celebrate the 75th Anniversary of the establishment of the tramway in 1885, Joe Franklin - General Manager - and his senior colleagues investigated what existed to represent this triumph of 'Progress'.

I remember visiting Copse Road Depot in Fleetwood - used by the Permanent Way gang - to see the ancient trams stored in there. Much to my surprise Mr Franklin arrived to look at Dreadnought 59, which had survived in response to a public appeal following the withdrawal of the class after the 1934 Season. He also examined the old Blackpool & Fleetwood crossbench car of 1898, numbered 127, and even 'toast-rack' 163 of 1927. At Bispham Depot - even more amazing - was one of the 1885 ex-conduit cars, which had survived as an overhead-line works car until 1934. To complete the quartet of historic cars, the Tramroad saloon car of 1914 was standing in Rigby Road Depot, for use by the depot staff as a restroom. Thus the 75th Anniversary was to be correctly represented by one of the founding 1885 trams, a famous 1902 successor, and a pair of Tramroad Company trams inherited by Blackpool Corporation in 1920.

Restoration of the vintage cars took place in the Central Works, commencing in December 1959 when Dreadnought 59 was towed back by a railcoach in the secrecy of a night-time. However, crossbench car 127, which had been used by the track gang, was driven under its own power to the Works in February 1960. Remarkably also driven under its own power, at 8 am on 25 February came the 1885 car from Bispham Depot. This went to show how the founder of the tram fleet had survived, spirited and agile! The final member of the quartet - Box car 40 - was driven the short distance from the Depot to the Body Shop, and the progress was secure.

It is interesting to record that the Body Shop foreman, Bert Kirby, had worked his time as an apprentice upon historic trams of this type, so commenced the restoration with experience! By 26 April the Dreadnought had left the Body Shop under power for the Paint Shop, and the others followed. Here they were transported by the tramcar traverser, which moved them sideways into position. Of the historic quartet, 1 and 59 were painted in the Municipal fleet livery of red and white, while 2 and 40 were painted in the Company livery of brown and cream. To everyone's surprise, in June the colourful quartet appeared in the Depot, providing a contrast with their more streamlined successors.

The debut event of the Anniversary Year took place on 15 June, when Dreadnought 59 was restored to the Promenade for the benefit of the press and the public. Together with Tramroad crossbench car No 2, it operated on the Promenade Circular Tour, in company with the Boat cars, and they captured the popularity of the public. The delightful ride upon an open-topper and a crossbench car also restored the 'One of the Joys of Life' phrase.

The full quartet made their maiden trip together on Wednesday 29 June, when passengers were carried on a sample Circular journey to Little Bispham. The 1885 car was withdrawn from service after a short period because it was considered 'too petite' for safety in the Sixties. Saloon car 40 was sent as a 'special' to Fleetwood on Market Days, and ran at speeds that equalled its modern counterparts. On 5 August No 40 collided with a lorry at a Thornton Gate road crossing, but only suffered slight damage because of its driver's swift use of the electric brake. From Sunday 31 July until Friday 5 August, No 59 became the 'Daily Mirror Tram', when all the fares were collected for charity. While 59 retained its historic appearance, its adverts were colourful and striking for the occasion.

Thus came the anniversary of the foundation day itself on 29 September, when a procession was staged along the Promenade, showing the whole development of the tramway fleet from 1885 to 1960. Appropriately No 1 led the two parades at 10.45 am and 3.00 pm, contrasting with new trailer-tram 276-T3 of 1960 bringing up the rear. When the trams lined up at the Pleasure Beach loop, the fleet was represented by trams belonging to their respective depots: for example, 1928 Pantograph car 170 from Bispham Depot, and Boat car 236 of 1934 with Standard 40 of 1924 from Marton Depot. It was amusing that 170 had no Promenade destinations on its indicator when it worked to the Pleasure Beach for the first time that day!

All were later ordered by age, except for the two 40s, which were the wrong way round, with 1924 before 1914. However, the first six historic cars showed the evolution by design through to the streamlined fleet of the Thirties. This was represented by railcoach 217, Boat car 236 and Balloon 249, followed by post-war Coronation 321 of 1953 and the Twin car 276-T3 of 1960.

The public were allowed to travel free of charge, and naturally they first occupied all the six historic cars, being a novelty to them rather than the routine service cars. Television filmed the procession to Little Bispham, where the trams posed on the turning circle, then returned to Blackpool where they unloaded at Talbot Square and returned to depot for lunch. The six historic cars, with the Pantograph and Boat car, were kept clean at Rigby Road Depot until they returned to the Pleasure Beach for the second procession at 3.00 pm. Unusually the routine was followed again until it was complete by 4.00 pm, when all the trams went into special service, apart from the veteran No 1.

Above **This Is It! The 1885 tram appropriately heads the Anniversary procession of vintage trams past the famous Tower, which opened in 1894.** *Evening Gazette, Blackpool*

There is no doubt that this memorable event established Blackpool Tramway as unique in celebrating its 75th Anniversary, and everyone imagined that the tramway would survive for ever! However, as an anti-climax on 7 October it emerged that the Transport Committee had decided to close the Squires Gate route in 1961, followed by the other street routes in 1962 and 1963. But it must be said that the 1960 celebration was exclusively for the Promenade tramway, which survived to reach its Centenary in 1985, making history once again!

Right **75 years apart - as the smart and diminutive car No 1 leaves Little Bispham loop, it draws level with the 12th car in the procession - T3 - new in 1960!** *Geoff Hyde*

Restoring the historic survivors

Above The Dreadnought survived at Copse Road Depot in Fleetwood, looking fairly antique and neglected! *R. P. Fergusson*

Below It was joined by Tramroad crossbench car 127 - originally 2 - used by the track gangs for transport, suitably in summer! *R. P. Fergusson*

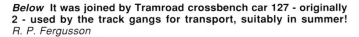

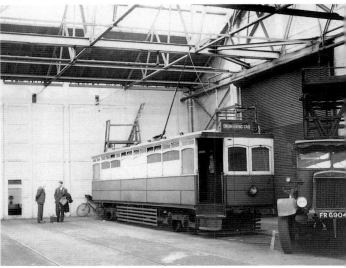

Top At Bispham Depot hid the 1885 tram No 4, which had been used as an overhead line works tram between the wars, and could still travel under its own power in 1960! *R. P. Fergusson*

Above The Tramroad saloon car 5 - formerly 40 - was used as a staff-room in Rigby Road Depot, and for transportation of the tower wagon when working on the overhead line. *R. P. Fergusson*

In the Body Shop, January to May 1960.
During their restoration the historic cars
added a charming air of antiquity to the
Body Shop of the Works. This first photograph, of Dreadnought 59 and crossbench 127, could have been taken 40
years earlier, but was taken in February
1960. *Author*

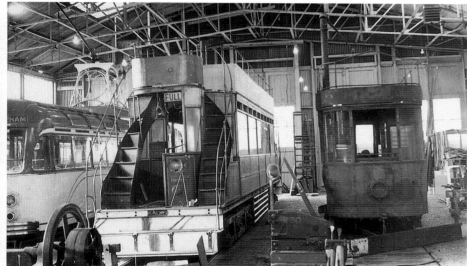

Later that month the Dreadnought was
joined by the 1885 car for restoration to
its original appearance without its working snowplough and vestibules. It can be
seen how the Dreadnought has been fitted with new platform steps, handrails
and decency panels along the top-deck -
and it is showing 'FULL'! Its neighbour is
a Brush railcar of 1937, a streamliner in
contrast to its predecessor. *Author*

By May 1960 considerable rebuilding
work has taken place on the 1885 car, featuring a new open platform with curved
dash and stairs to the top deck. Here the
handrails are fitted with modesty panelling, in keeping with its age, while the
saloon has been refitted with a solid side
upon the removal of the delivery door.
Alongside is the Box saloon car of 1914 -
No 40 - in need of remedial body repairs
of a minimal nature. *Author*

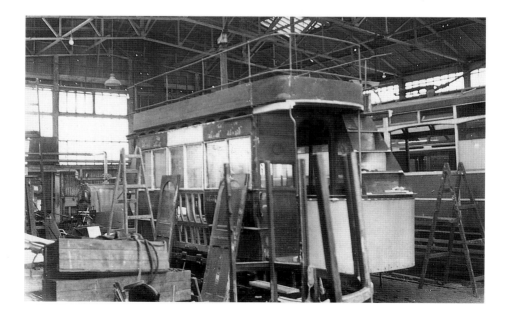

In the Paint Shop in May 1960 the Dreadnought is receiving the Corporation livery of red and white, achieved by researching the dark paint still clinging to its original panels at each end, and mixing post office red with maroon. The side teak panels were rubbed down and varnished, complete with white lining and two Municipal coats of arms with the green garter of the Thirties. The seats on the top deck were newly made, and were varnished to match the traditional panelling. The white saloon window frames and stair panels were lined in red, while the stair risers had black kicking-plates. *Author*

An altogether striking and noble appearance also applied to 1885 car No 1, which was really No 4! Two men are seen busily at work on this car: the upper is apparently painting the handrails, while the lower man repaints the four-wheel truck and lifeguard, dark brown in colour. *Author*

The third of the historic trio in the Paint Shop is crossbench car 127, which will be correctly numbered 2 in the Tramroad Company fleet of 1898. The livery starts with white on the roof, varnished pillars to the open saloon, and a black advertising panel. That only leaves the dash-panel, which will be repainted in the Company livery of chocolate, complete with white running boards along the side, but a red kicking-plate, for a warning effect! *Author*

BLACKPOOL TRAMS 1950-1966

Above 'Ye Olde Dreadnought - Built for Blackpool 1901' announces the display panel of 59 when it returns to active life in the tram depot once more in June 1960. By comparison with Coronation 316 of 1953 in the background, there is no doubt that the old Promenade open-topper is impressive, and with its full-width steps and curved railings it will embrace its customers in large numbers! It reminds us of the old days, when the Dreadnoughts loaded and unloaded simultaneously - the original 'passenger flow'! *Author*

Left 'This Is It! - The First Electric Street Tramcar in England' - No 1 of 1885, looking quite miniature, and with a long trolley pole to reach the overhead; the original conduit tramcars were converted to the overhead line with the tramway system in 1899. Consequently the tram is 75 years old, but not the trolley. *A. D. Packer collection*

Above The Blackpool & Fleetwood Tramroad pair on display outside the depot in their chocolate and cream livery and their Company fleet numbers: No 2 of 1898 and 40 of 1914. The oldest carriess the slogan 'The First Tramway from Blackpool to Fleetwood', and 40 'A Saloon Tramride from Blackpool to Fleetwood'. They share the characteristic of a long wheelbase, giving a smooth ride along the coastal tramway on an inter-urban route in the American tradition. *R. P. Fergusson*

57

Vintage Coastal Tour

On 9 July 1960 the Tramway Museum Society organised a first tour on the vintage cars. They are seen here at Starr Gate, ready to turn on the loop and commence the historic journey to Fleetwood. The 1898 Tramroad car 2 leads, followed by Dreadnought 59, but the rear No 1 gains all the attention of the crowd of enthusiasts! *Author*

No 1 'loops the loop' round the turning circle for the first time, watched and filmed by its fans - luckily the trolley can reach the overhead! Nobody was allowed on the top deck, for safety reasons. *Author*

At Bispham Station the three vintage trams stand on the centre line, allowing the service cars to pass on each side. The following Coronation 318, bound for Cleveleys, provides a contrast with its predecessors. All the enthusiasts are standing on the cliffs to get this elevated view, with the hotels in the background. No 1, being left here, was banned from travelling further north - without precedent! *Author*

BLACKPOOL TRAMS 1950-1966

No 2 arrives at Fleetwood Ferry for the first time, because in Company days it turned round at Bold Street. Its driver - Jimmy Booth - poses in front of the tram for the benefit of the crowd. The holiday-makers at the tram stop are surprised, and would no doubt like to ride back to Blackpool on No 2 - but it is 'RESERVED'. *Author*

Returning to Bispham at speed in the tra-ditional Tramroad manner - the enthusi-asts can then return to No 1, which has been waiting here. Such a sunny day made riding on the open cars perfect, in contrast to the passing 1953 Coronation 313! *A. D. Packer collection*

No 1 stops in front of Derby Baths, where its passengers can change cars and take a photograph. Is somebody heading for the Boat car in front? The driver is look-ing down at his feet on the bell pedal, but his hands are firmly on the controller and hand-brake handles. *R. P. Fergusson*

Above At Fleetwood Ferry Box car 40 contrasts with Coronation car 318 as they stand side by side on Market Day. Note that the driver stands to drive 40, while he sits comfortably to operate the accelerator stick on 318. Passengers board 40 up three steps at the corner entrance, and the saloon is high off the ground - better for a longer coastal ride, and it can go fast too! *Author*

Left In front of the Tower No 2 is attracting passengers on the Promenade Circular Tour, while the railcoach from Squires Gate to Bispham passes it on the loop line. While the July weather is so sunny the Promenade is full of strolling holidaymakers - some would enjoy a ride on an open car for fresh air! *David Packer collection*

Dreadnought 59 beside the sea on the Queens Promenade in August 1960 while it was sponsored by the *Daily Mirror*, and all the fares were given to charity. Followed by the mundane service cars of the streamline era, the striking appearance of the Dreadnought is outstanding. It was unique with its central driver surrounded by twin staircases to the open-top deck and the broad steps across the front - passengers entered from the rear of the tram. The design had been bought by Blackpool from Mr Shrewsbury of Camberwell in 1897, and retained it exclusively to their 20 Dreadnoughts. Survivor 59 received acclaim and became popular with the public - perhaps all 20 should have been retained in 1934! *Author*

The interior saloon as restored to its original condition in 1960, with beautiful varnished teak woodwork, bevelled mirrors and panels in the partition, and the curved ribs of the ceiling. The latter conceal the quarter lights that give air and light above the plate-glass windows. It is interesting to note the curved handrail, which originally also carried standee handles. There is also a leather strap along the ceiling, pulled to ring the bell and signal to the driver. Forty-nine passengers sat 'outside' on the top deck, and 37 in the saloon, half upon reversing seats and half upon longitudinal seating facing inwards - a good 86 passengers seated! *Author*

The 75th Anniversary

No 1, in position at the Pleasure Beach on the afternoon of 29 September 1960, prepares to commemorate the first Promenade journey on the same day in 1885. *Graham Weaver*

The six historic trams, half of which have a Promenade tradition - 1, 59 and Standard 40 - and half are single-deckers of the Tramroad - 2, 40 and 170. It is interesting to note that 170 is in daily service on the Fleetwood route, and has no Promenade destinations! *Graham Weaver*

Here is one of the lengthy stops at North Pier for the press and newsreel photographers, with passengers still in place on the trams! There is a queue waiting to board any trams with empty seats from South Shore. *Graham Weaver*

procession, 1960

A Dreadnought passenger's view on Little Bispham loop, showing the 1885 car followed by No 2 full of passengers, while the official photographers are mounted on the tower-wagon on the extreme right to take photographs of the occasion. Sadly no passengers were allowed on the upper deck of No 1. *Graham Weaver*

Looking from the balcony of 40 we can see Box 40, Pantograph 170, Railcoach 217 and the front of Boat 236 - all full of passengers who were not allowed to leave their trams in the procession. *Graham Weaver*

On the return journey the procession reaches Gynn Square, where Dreadnought 59 is seen followed by Standard 40 with the Savoy Hotel in the background. A passing Balloon - heading north - conceals the other 40, but not quite 170 and 236. *Graham Weaver*

BECAUSE it is a holiday resort, Blackpool's trams have provided a Circular Tour, Coastal Tour and Tour of the Illuminations.

The Circular Tour

The Circular Tour has a long tradition in this century, using toast-racks to carry sightseeing holidaymakers round the town of Blackpool, starting in 1911. Initially the Tour started in Talbot Square outside the Clifton Hotel, which was also terminus of the Marton route. When fully loaded, the toast-racks crossed to the Promenade, travelled as far as South Pier, turned up Station Road to Lytham Road, Royal Oak, then travelled round the Marton route and so back to Talbot Square. When the new South Promenade was opened by Lord Derby in 1926, the Circular Tour was extended as far as Starr Gate, and turned into Squires Gate Lane on the southern border with Lytham St Annes. It then travelled along Lytham Road as far as Royal Oak, giving the passengers a longer ride.

When the new open Boat trams arrived in 1934, they became the second generation of trams on the Circular Tour. In April 1937 the blue-cars of Lytham St Annes, which operated from their depot in Squires Gate Lane, were replaced by buses. Blackpool negotiated for the use of the northern track for Circular Tour trams, although they briefly used both tracks in Squires Gate Lane for service trams, until they were charged by Lytham St Annes.

Following the start of the Second World War in 1939 there was a cessation of the Circular Tour until 1957, when the Blackpool track was uncovered, enabling the Boat trams to resume the tradition. In the season the

'Queue Here - Tour Takes Approx One Hour.' The open Boat trams are lined up in Talbot Square, filling with passengers before setting off on their voyage. These open trams were fittingly named 'Boat cars', their profile resembling that of their floating cousins! Delightfully they have a 'sea wave' on their 'bows' - in the green and cream livery - and an elegant canopy over the centre platform surmounted by the trolley tower. Each Boat car is dressed overall by a string of coloured lights from the tower to a mast in each corner. *Author*

open Boat trams lined up in Talbot Square, advertised by their poster 'Take the Circular Tour Round Blackpool, 1/3d'. Away from the Promenade, mingling with the busy service cars on the street routes, the open Circular Tour Boats looked quite unusual, and they had to keep up speed so as not to delay the three-minute service! For the passengers it was an opportunity to see the interesting parts of the town, while enjoying the sunshine. Of course riding on an open Boat tram was delightful in the warm sun, but if it came on to rain the passengers got wet - a Boat has been seen standing empty in the middle of Clifton Drive while they took refuge in the Starr Gate tram shelter! In order to return quickly to Talbot Square, the driver drove at speed along Lytham Road, while the passengers crowded under the platform canopy for shelter. You never knew your luck on a Circular Tour!

In 1960, when the four vintage trams were restored for the 75th Anniversary of the tramway, a new Promenade Circular was operated by the 1898 Tramroad crossbench tramcar and 1902 open-top Dreadnought. They loaded at the Tower and travelled northwards to Little Bispham, circled round the loop, as befitted a Circular Tour, and returned southbound to Pleasure Beach. There the passengers could enjoy different angles of the view, including South Shore open-air baths, as the tram circled to return to the Tower. The Boat cars were also used on the Promenade Circular, getting ready for the closure of the Lytham Road route in 1961 when the traditional Circular Tour via Marton would finally finish.

While the Circular Tour was ideal for the general public, the tram enthusiasts organised their own tours using a variety of popular trams. Riding on vintage trams for the 75th Anniversary, they travelled the length of the Coastal Tour and the width of the Circular Tour, reaching every part of the town! To the surprise of the travelling public, waiting for their familiar service trams, they would appear loaded with enthusiasts, and some scenes are included in the following pages.

The duty Inspector blows his whistle for the Boat to start, the conductor rings the electric bell for the driver, and the tram crosses the carriageway to the Promenade. A duty Special Constable halts the traffic and gives the tram clearance. Leaving Talbot Square they say goodbye to the Midland Bank, Nutbrown Arcade and Booth's grocery and are on the lookout for different sights. On the Promenade tramway the driver of the Boat car must give way to the service trams en route to Starr Gate and Squires Gate, and yet he doesn't have to stop en route! *David Packer collection*

Once the open Boat trams used to take a Circular round the streets of Blackpool, but were redirected in 1961 along the coast. Joining the passengers on a Sunday morning we see the lovely view from the Boat car looking towards Norbreck. The passengers enjoy the ride, but the little boy on the right looks round to see the photographer - funny, it's the conductor! When we reach Little Bispham the conductor will turn the points for the Circular loop line and will signal to the driver with his whistle. *Author*

The open-top Dreadnought gave passengers a splendid view of the Promenade scene - unless it rained. Then they could enter the splendid Tower building for dancing in the magnificent Ballroom to Reginald Dixon playing the Wurlitzer. Two conduc- tors are needed on a double-deck tram at Blackpool, seen here on the Dreadnought platform. One collects fares on the top deck, while the other looks after the lower saloon and signals the driver. *R. P. Fergusson*

For the 75th Anniversary of the tramway in 1960, historic trams were introduced to the Promenade Circular, loading at the Tower. There were two types of tram in use: the 1898 Blackpool & Fleetwood crossbench car and the 1902 open-top Dreadnought. While waiting for the Tour to start, passengers could sit and read the advertising boards on the Tower building: Menagerie, Aquarium, Roof Gardens and Zoo. The conductor collects the fares from the passengers, while the driver - Albert Booth - waits for more cus- tomers to fill the tram before he sets off on the Circular. *R. P. Fergusson*

BLACKPOOL TRAMS 1950-1966

Going northbound first, the crossbench car has reached Little Bispham loop, circled round and now returns southbound. This open-sided tram is fitted with a wooden rail that is lowered at each side for safety, to keep the passengers in their seats. The driver stands upright to handle the controller and the handbrake mounted on the front dash. The conductor moves along the tram using the foot-board, collecting the fares. *R. P. Fergusson*

The open-top Dreadnought on the Promenade Circular advertises The Milk Race, which started and finished at Blackpool, organised by the Milk Board. The passengers are passing the splendid Derby Baths where swimmers could enjoy themselves, and others train for Olympic Games. The Derby Baths were opened and named in 1939 by Lord Derby, who previously in 1926 had opened Stanley Park. The tram on the Promenade Circular did not need to obey the tram stop signs 'Cars Stop By Request'. *Author*

By 1964 one of the great sights on the Promenade Circular was the construction of Lewis's Store, a new neighbour of the Tower. Meanwhile the 'Wonderland of the World' advertises the Tower Circus, the 'Tower Children's Review' and Charles Barlow & His Band. *Author*

Left 'Cars Stop By Request' at Foxhall, but the horse with its landau ignores the passing Boat car and tucks into its lunch! The landau driver relaxes and turns his back upon the tramway scene, unless some passengers are willing to ride in style. The landaus are a vintage form of cab along the Promenade in the Season. *A. D. Packer collection*

Below The Boat car continues towards South Pier on the Tour, passing the Queens Hotel in 1954. It is a fine day and the holidaymakers enjoy the beach on deckchairs, hired from the deckchair man on the Prom. There are one or two boat rides, paddling in the sea and a Punch & Judy show. Looking along the sea front, the landing-stage of North Pier in the distance outstretches Central Pier. *Valentine & Sons, Dundee*

BLACKPOOL TRAMS 1950-1966

The Dreadnought's Promenade Circular reaches the Pleasure Beach turning loop, passing a new trailer twin-car unit. The elevated passengers get a good view of the Pleasure Beach, with the impressive Casino building, the twin big wheels and Noah's Ark. The conductor switches the points so the tram can turn right and take the loop to return to the Tower. *Author*

During an evening tour on 22 May 1961 by Boat 229, the sunshine casts long shadows on the loop line. The sight of the Casino as the passengers approach provides them with a good impression of the Thirties - in 1939 it came as the climax of the modernisation of the Pleasure Beach, in those years immediately before the war. A Circular Tour poster is mounted above the 'CARS STOP HERE' sign, but Tours don't stop here! *Author*

Tramway enthusiasts enjoyed their own tours on the same route, using vintage trams like Standard car 40, significantly standing at the junction of the track to St Annes. They would have enjoyed the route in pre-war years, but it is clear that by 1959 there is no longer an overhead line. *Author*

Left A Circular Tour for tram enthusiasts, using two single-deckers, is passing Woodheads Garage, main dealers for Singer and Hillman cars, while a Morris Minor gets its petrol. The vintage Rlackpool & Fleetwood Pantograph cars are overtaken by a blue Lytham St Annes bus heading for Blackpool. *Author*

Below At the junction with Squires Gate Lane, the tram track diverts: left for the Circular Tour and right to St Annes, where the blue-cars journeyed until 1937, when they were replaced by buses. The passengers on the Circular Tour see the Squires Gate Inn and pass Nicholson's shop, where 'Sunglasses our Speciality'. A sign directs visitors to Billy Smart's Circus - an annual visit! *Author*

BLACKPOOL TRAMS 1950-1966

Right Once in Squires Gate Lane the trams mount the railway bridge and provide a good view of the Airport, hangars and aircraft factory. On the right-hand side is the former tram depot of Lytham St Annes, now used by their buses. The 'bungalow' on the extreme right contains the Transport Offices and a room for the General Manager. The track still used by the Circular Tour tram is clear, while the westbound track is covered by tarmac and unusable, although it still has an overhead line! *Author*

Below Moments after the picture on page 11 was taken, the touring double-decker Balloon tram swings round the curve from Squires Gate Lane into Lytham Road, opposite the Airport entrance, in May 1959, still pursued by the two boys on their bikes! *R. P. Fergusson*

Above The Boat car on the Circular has reached the Saddle Inn, advertising C&S Ales, but the driver cannot stop for a visit! He looks round and sees the Marton service car following them, which means that the Boat has to keep floating ahead towards the Town Centre! *R. P. Fergusson*

Below A diversion from the Circular Tour would be a visit to South Pier via Station Road, where we see the two vintage trams and a crowd of tram enthusiasts. This is the terminus for the Marton trams and buses on route 23, one of which is advertising C&S Ales, as well as 'Ardron's for Hardware'. *Author*

Right In this scene a vintage Southampton tram has been driven out of Marton Depot following presentation to the new Tramway Museum Society, whose members are on the open top deck. Modern service car 208 passes on its way to Royal Oak via Marton, and its driver sits comfortably to drive this tram with its windscreen open on a warm sunny day in 1955. *Dennis Gill*

Below To complete the Circular Tour of the town the trams returned through the Town Centre. Here vintage Standard tram 41, on another enthusiasts' tour, passes the Opera House in Church Street, where 'The Big Show of 1958' is taking place twice nightly at 6.15 and 8.50. David Whitfield - the great singer - leads the cast, and his neighbour at the Winter Gardens is comedienne Hylda Baker - 'She Knows Y'Know'. The passengers will disembark in Talbot Square when their Circular ends. *A. D. Packer collection*

BLACKPOOL TRAMS 1950-1966   73

The Coastal Tour

The Coastal Tour commenced in 1958 with the introduction of a new trailer tram, 276 & 275: 'Twenty Two Miles, Fare 3/-, To & From Blackpool and Fleetwood'. While this was a great novelty, it proved too long for holidaymakers, who were unable to have a break at Fleetwood Ferry. When the ten new trailer trams were delivered in 1960, the Coastal Tour did not retain the popularity of the Circular Tour.

Above Coastal Tour passengers were taken to Fleetwood, where the tram is seen arriving on its inaugural visit with civic passengers, including the Mayors of Blackpool, Fleetwood and Cleveleys. This was 9 April 1958, and all is quiet on the Ferry scene. The new twin-car has parked on the siding to allow the Blackpool & Fleetwood service cars to pass. *R. P. Fergusson*

Below A lovely view from Standard 41 of the new twin-set 276 & 275 on the Coastal Tour on the Promenade in 1958. In an all-cream livery, it contrasts with the double-decker Balloons behind, which are in the post-war green livery. While South Pier is familiar, can you recognise the Lost Children's Centre bus on the sea front? It is a 1937 Leyland Tiger! *Dennis Gill*

TRAMS IN LIGHTS - THE GREATEST FREE SHOW ON EARTH

THE origins of illuminated trams date back to the Diamond Jubilee of Queen Victoria in 1897, and the Coronations of King Edward VII in 1902 and King George V in 1911. However, the Illuminations themselves were founded in 1912, when Princess Louise opened Princess Parade round the sea side of the Metropole Hotel. The first regular illuminated tram - De Luxe 68 - celebrated that occasion and the visit of King George and Queen Mary in 1913, followed by the Autumn Illuminations.

There was an interlude during the First World War and the post-war Carnivals, until the Autumn Illuminations were revived in 1925 with the launching of the newly created Gondola tram. The crew had to be dressed as Gondoliers, but did not carry any passengers - only a small orchestra playing Gilbert & Sullivan's *The Gondoliers*! In the following year the Lifeboat was launched and named 'The Jubilee' to commemorate the 50th Jubilee of Blackpool Borough. In 1937 a trio was created with the Bandwagon, to represent the concept of a tram in 2037. During the Second World War - while the Gondola and Lifeboat were stored - the Bandwagon was used for advertising fund-raising efforts, culminating in VE and VJ Day in 1945.

The triumph came in 1949 when the Illuminations were restored again, using the tableaux stored during the war, and happiness was celebrated once again! The illuminated tramway trio returned to the Lights, the renamed Progress car assuming the form of a surreptitious double-

decker with silhouette passengers and loudly broadcast music. Every year the illuminated trio toured the inland parts of the town on the last Saturday of the Illuminations, visiting Squires Gate, Marton and North Station, but not Fleetwood. They became a familiar source of attention, but never carried passengers - except a special guest such as the Duke of Kent in 1937. He used the Lifeboat, while the Gondola transported the artist who switched on the Illuminations each year.

In 1959 a new tradition was started with the launching of the passenger-carrying 'paddle-steamer' Blackpool Belle, which replaced the Progress car. The Gondola and Lifeboat were given gang-planks that could be lowered from their sides to admit their passengers. The first of a new post-war generation, Blackpool Belle was created from 1927 toast-rack 163; it looked colourful and was heard musically as it passed through the Illuminations.

With the retirement of the elderly Lifeboat in 1961 and Gondola in 1962, which simulated pitching and tossing ships, they were replaced by a new generation of the Rocket and Western Train respectively. The novelty of Tramnik One was enhanced by the saloon tilted at an angle of 20 degrees, which provided the passengers with a new angle on the Lights! The Santa Fe train was in the new generation of ten twin-cars, introduced in 1960 and using their towing gear. By 1962 the new trio of illuminated trams were being widely admired, contributing mobile tableaux to the Illuminations scene.

The Illuminations in pre-war years at Talbot Square, showing the first illuminated De-Luxe tram with the slogan 'Long Live Our King & Queen in Health & Happiness' for their visit in 1913. The style of the Lights was more primitive then, during that initial foundation of the tradition of Lights each year. *Author's collection*

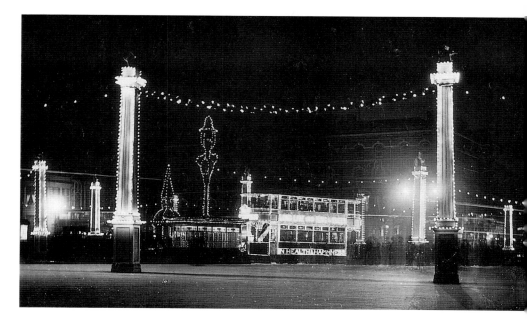

Post-war restoration of the Lights

Above An evening view of Talbot Square in 1950, with the Marton tram standing next to the illuminated shelter in the centre of the Square. The Town Hall looks striking, its profile lit by columns of lights, the coat of arms on display and the tower floodlit. The Clifton Hotel, Yates's Wine Lodge and the Midland Bank are also floodlit, while strings of lights surround the Square and along Clifton Street and Talbot Road. *Baron-Hartley, Blackpool*

Left Here is a splendid view of the switch-on of the 1953 Illuminations, with the illuminated Gondola and Lifeboat travelling through the enormous crowd on the Promenade. The switch-on was performed by George Formby, the latest in a long line of famous people performing this service each year. The Clifton Hotel looks impressive, its floodlights making it stand out in the darkness. An open Boat car and railcoaches have their trolley towers illuminated, but are upstaged by the Lights trams. Many cars are queuing in the carriageway, together with service bus 22A for Cleveleys. *Author's collection*

Above The Gondola - one of the most elegant illuminated trams in the history of the Illuminations - was built upon one of the original 1901 Marton four-wheel trams, No 28. The side panels show the lines of the timber beneath a coat of painted canvas, bearing the Seagull from Blackpool's arms carrying the motto 'Progress'. The graceful 'pagoda' roof is lined by coloured bulbs, while the wax curtains are floodlit for elegance. The driver stands behind the railings, and has to allow for the length of the high prow in front of him while driving. Sadly in 1962 the Gondola met its end when it collided with another tram, but has never been forgotten!
Author's collection

Below The Lifeboat 'Jubilee' marked the 50th Anniversary of Blackpool Borough in 1926, when the new South Promenade was opened by Lord Derby. It followed the design of a lifeboat in its dark blue and white livery, with its body having rowlocks and safety rope loops along the side. Placed centrally was a mast for the sails, concealing the trolley pole; the illuminated sails could be reversed to be in the right position for the direction in which the tram was travelling. On the bows you may notice the official coat of arms, surrounded by a red garter reading 'Blackpool Corporation Jubilee'. The public admired this tram as it pitched and rolled over the tramway, resembling a real lifeboat at sea, until 1961, when it retired. *Author's collection*

Above The Progress illuminated car of 1949, depicting a gigantic Municipal coat of arms, passes through the crowd, many thousand strong, for the switch-on in 1953. It gives a brilliant halo of light and moves to a loud tune, and Talbot Square provides an attractive setting, with Yates's Wine Lodge as a centrepiece. However, the Marton trams are obviously absent from their terminus, and must be turning in Abingdon Street. *Author's collection*

Left 'We Are Happy to Entertain - In Sunshine, Wind or Rain.' It looks as though passengers are sitting in the saloon of an illuminated double-decker, but this tram was built on the wooden frame of an 1899 crossbench car in 1937 as the Bandwagon. Rebuilt as the Progress car for the 1949 Illuminations, it was promoted to this handsome form as a streamliner design of the Thirties. Its decoration came to a climax in 1958 when one side showed a tableau of Columbus's *Mayflower* of 1492. Sadly that was to be its finale. *Author's collection*

BLACKPOOL TRAMS 1950-1966

Above An autumn evening on 12 September 1959 on Central Promenade, where large crowds are strolling and waiting for the Illuminations switch-on. The open Boat car is heading for the Tower, while Balloon 244 shows 'FOOTBALL GROUND' on its indicators and is transporting supporters. It will turn left at Manchester Square and travel along Lytham Road towards the Blackpool Football Club in Bloomfield Road. Blackpool was the FA Cup winner in 1953 against Bolton FC, and has many followers! *Author*

Below A view along Princess Parade in the Fifties, with the tram track reflecting the light as a Coronation tram approaches. Butlins, on the right, now own the Metropole, and the ABC sign on the left marks the Princess Cinema, whose entrance is strongly illuminated! This street section of the Illuminations is decorated with strings of lights, but the Tower dominates the colourful scene. The copper wire of the tramway overhead reflects the lights and gleams in the dark to add to the effect. *Blackpool Publicity Department*

Televising the Illuminations

The televising of the Illuminations took place for the first time by the BBC in 1951, when the old toast-rack, 165, carried a mobile generator for two television cameras and a commentator. In 1953 a pair of toast-racks - 165 and 166 - were used together, with the first as camera studio and the second carrying the generator. Finally they were rebuilt in 1956, with 166 becoming a mobile studio with an elevated position of good vision for the commentator. The name 'BBC Television Service' on the side changed to ABC TV when that company used the television trams for *Holiday Parade* in 1961, but it fell into disuse after that. No 166 is now restored as a traditional toast-rack at the National Tramway Museum, Crich, Derbyshire, and the modern television broadcast does not need a special tramcar!

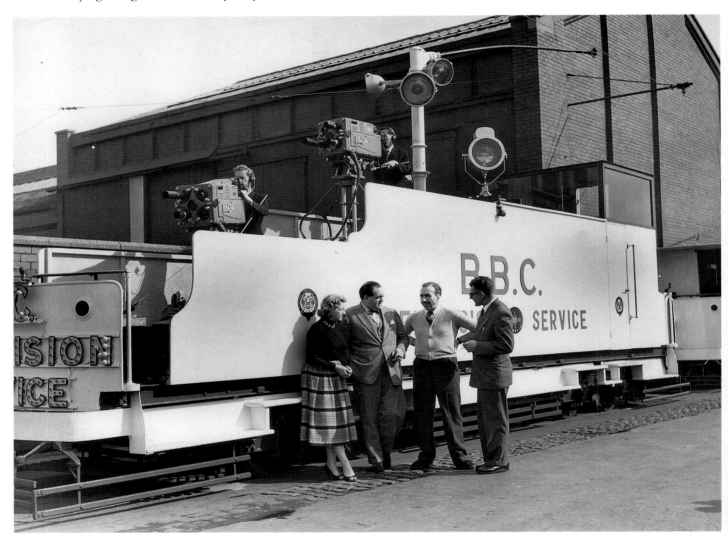

Above Toast-rack trams 166 and 165 in 1956, newly rebuilt for the BBC Television Service, with two television cameras and flood-lights on view in the first, and a generator hidden in the second. The famous commentator Richard Dimbleby and his wife are seen in front of the TV tram with Producer Barney Colehan and Publicity Officer Harry Porter. The elevated studio will enable Richard to gain a good view of the Illuminations for the television programme from Blackpool to follow. What a historic occasion! *Blackpool Publicity Department*

Above right In the daylight we see the Gondola and Lifeboat - along with the new Blackpool Belle in the background - outside the tram depot in Hopton Road. Unfortunately they don't look as striking as when illuminated at night, but their profile is a novelty to the passers-by. A policeman calls at the boarding-house on business, while the cars and a Bedford Dormobile stand clear of the tram track. *R. P. Fergusson*

Right This autumn 1959 view in the depot shows the illuminated tram fleet: Blackpool Belle, Gondola, Lifeboat and Standard 158. They are ready to leave the depot in the evening to tour round the Lights, but why does 158 show 'LAYTON' on its screen? The clean inspection pits in the foreground enable staff to examine the underneath of a tram, and check the brake-shoes. The new Belle's elegant appearance dominates the scene, with a large fleet of Balloon double-deckers in the background. *Author*

BLACKPOOL TRAMS 1950-1966

BLACKPOOL TRAMS 1950-1966

Left With 'Tour of the Illuminations' on its indicator Standard 159 arrives at Central Station fully illuminated. In its traditional form - along with 158 - its profile is lined with lights, but during the day operates as a 'Special' along the Promenade. The lights can be turned on at night during the summer to announce 'Welcome to Blackpool Illuminations' and the dates each year. Along with other traditional trams, the last three Standards ran for the final time in 1966, when they retired to tramway museums in the UK and USA. *R. P. Fergusson*

Below left The newly built Blackpool Belle in 1959, showing its delightful form as a paddle-steamer in the American style, and fly-ing the Union Jack and Stars and Stripes. Built on the old toast-rack 163, the structure had a wooden frame and panelling, with an illuminated interior behind the coloured windows. The driver sat in an enclosed cab - for comfort - while the 32 passengers sat along the open 'deck' of the steamboat. The paddles appeared to revolve with fluorescent tubes attached, and sea-coloured lights around the hull gave the impression of sailing. In the centre of the top deck was the funnel, concealing the trolley pole, the top of which could be reversed. The first passenger was the famous American actress Jayne Mansfield, who switched on the 1959 Lights. Blackpool Belle sailed until 1978, and is now in Glenwood Trolley Park, Oregon, USA - its native land? *E. R. Hargreaves*

Above Tramnik One was built in 1961 upon the frame of Pantograph 168, to commemorate the first man in space, Russia's Yuri Gargarin. The 46 passengers board through the 'rocket jets' at the back, and find that the saloon is tilted at 20 degrees. Thus they are secured in their hard-to-reach seats and look forward towards the 'cockpit' with its twin pilots - waxworks in space out-fits! The tram driver sits in his own cab beneath the rocket's fuse-lage, and his conductor signals by electric buzzer. You will have to count or guess how many thousand bulbs light up the Rocket and flicker on its jet fuselage. *Newspix, Blackpool*

A new generation of illuminated trams

A Tour of the Illuminations is a fine tradition of the tramway, which in the Fifties produced queues at Bispham, Central Station and North Pier. Double-deckers were always used, including the vintage Standards from Marton Depot, which provided upstairs passengers with an elevated view. Those who wished to travel on the illu-minated trams - Western Train, Tramnik One or Blackpool Belle - queued at North Pier, paid a higher fare and received a souvenir ticket: 'Souvenir Ticket of the Greatest Free Show on Earth'. In 1963 the Hovertram was added to the fleet, 50 feet long with accommodation for 99 passengers, 42 of them are on the upper deck where panoramic windows gave unrestricted views. The conclu-sion came in 1965 when the last Pantograph tram 170 was rebuilt as the frigate 'HMS Blackpool': 'The model frigate is another example of the ingenuity of the craftsmen in the Transport Department'. Throughout the Illuminations era the tradition has continued - and to this day you can always enjoy seeing the illuminated trams if you visit Blackpool in the autumn.

Above The Western Train is seen here in daylight during the Summer Season of 1963 on the Promenade, on a limited-stop service from Little Bispham. It is notable that ABC Weekend Television were first to sponsor an illuminated tram, and others followed. You can see the logs on top of the tender, from where springs the trolley pole of Tramroad tradition! *Author*

Below When you are out for a walk along the Central Promenade in 1963 with your mother, you could get surprised by a Western Train! Here it is seen on a Circular Tour along the Golden Mile, and looks different from the trailer trams in the daylight. It does use the same equipment, but doesn't sound similar with its brass bell - clang, clang, clang! *Author*

Undoubtedly the largest and most memorable illuminated tram, in the form of an American Santa Fe locomotive with carriage, was built in 1962. The locomotive was constructed upon railcoach 209, and the trailer from Pantograph 174. It features a large smoke-stack, cow-catcher and brass bell for signalling. The driver sits in the glass-fronted 'smokebox' and uses the traditional controller and air-brakes; the train can be driven in reverse from the trailer, when returning to the depot. It can carry 95 passengers, 35 in the locomotive 'tender' and 60 in the carriage. *Newspix, Blackpool*

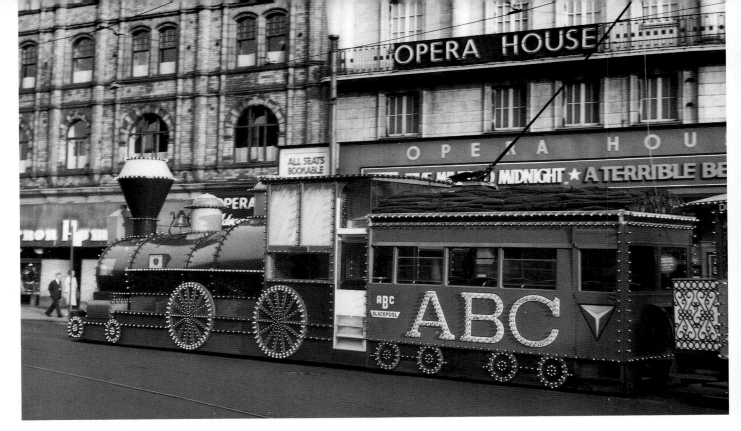

It is just as unusual to see a locomotive in the Town Centre, indeed any tram, since the Marton route finished in 1962 and the date of this photograph is 31 May 1963. However, this is a famous occasion - the opening of the new ABC Theatre in Church Street. *Holiday Carnival* starred Cliff Richard and The Shadows, who featured in the opening ceremony, and here the Mayor arrives from the Town Hall by the Santa Fe Train. The public were thrilled to see the illuminated tram coming up the street, but when the trumpets were sounded for the Theatre opening, the tram reversed away quietly, back to its native Promenade. Thus it became the last tram in the Town Centre - we will remember it for ever!
Graham Weaver

Right 'That's Shell, That Was!' Shell sponsored the Hovertram when it joined the Illuminations in 1963, here seen with the Tower. Designed appropriately with 'jet engines' on the roof, the Hovertram was built upon 1934 railcoach 222. It has the largest capacity of 99 seats, all facing forward, with a low-bridge design upstairs like the old-style double-decker buses. The door is at the back of the tram, with stairs to the upper deck.
Evening Gazette, Blackpool

Below In 1965 a fifth member of the illuminated fleet was created from Pantograph 170, and designed as the frigate 'HMS Blackpool'. While having high bows and an accurate superstructure for a warship, the final illuminated tram is not as spectacular as the others, or as handsome as its predecessors. There is, however, a comfortable ride in the saloon, and the driver is sitting on the bridge and can sound a loud klaxon to frighten the pedestrians in his path!
Saidman Brothers, Blackpool

THE trams were and still are familiar to the public in all their shapes and forms, but not where they lived: DEPOT, as shown on their indicators. Having said that, it depended at which depot they are based: Marton cars showed 'DEPOT' and even 'MARTON DEPOT' (in Whitegate Drive), whereas Bispham Depot was hidden down Red Bank Road, so its trams showed '1 - BISPHAM' on their indicators. However, the large Central Depot off Lytham Road, built in 1935 and housing 100 trams, was reached by Squires Gate cars showing 'DEPOT', but Promenade cars showing 'MANCHESTER SQUARE'.

In addition to these three service depots, where trams were maintained mechanically and electrically as well as cleaned, there were two other tramway buildings for storage and works. Blundell Street Depot was the first for trams

Platform staff

Below Claude Lane standing at the controls of Standard 99 at Royal Oak in the Forties, while based on Marton Depot. *Author's collection*

Below right Margaret O'Farrell - the final wartime motorwoman - seated at the controls of a Coronation in 1965 at Rigby Road Depot. *Author's collection*

Bottom right Steve Palmer - one of the seasonal conductors of 1960-4 - standing in front of Brush car 284 from Bispham Depot. *Author's collection*

in 1885, and Copse Road Depot belonged to the Tramroad Company, and was used for the Permanent Way.

In the Fifties - until closure of Marton in 1962 and Bispham in 1963 - each depot had a family of platform staff headed by the Depot Inspector and a fraternity of engineering staff headed by the Superintendent. Without doubt the staff owed loyalty to their depot. Marton was in the suburbs of Blackpool, operating an independent route and Promenade 'Specials'; Bispham was known as 'the other Firm', dating back to Tramroad Company ownership, and operated the coastal inter-urban and the Squires Gate routes; Rigby Road was the Headquarters, with the Transport Offices, Works Buildings and the Central Depot, which operated the Promenade tram service to Fleetwood and shared the Squires Gate route. Of course all three depots supplied 'Specials' to the Prom.

Trams were allocated to the Depots by types: Marton had its own modern Vambacs, vintage Standards and the open Boat cars; Bispham had the Brush railcars and Pantograph cars; and both shared some railcoaches. The Central Depot had the new Coronations exclusively for seafront routes, Balloons for Squires Gate and the Promenade, and many railcoaches too. It is interesting to

note that three double-deckers were allocated to Marton Depot for school specials, but visited the Prom during the day. All its native trams were fitted with a swivel-head on their trolley, so that they could angle-work on sharp curves and use the Royal Oak trolley reverser!

Finally it is worth recording that Blundell Street Depot of 1885 was enlarged in 1898, and was used as the main depot until replaced by the new depot in 1935. Having been used as a bus garage in the Fifties, trams returned in March 1963 to compensate for the loss of Marton Depot. When trams travelled to the Promenade via Princess Street at Easter, the local residents protested, resulting in a new rear entrance at Rigby Road. The illuminated trams and vintage trams were stored there too - good company!

Depots

It's 12.05 at Marton Depot, and Boat car 227 has been brought outside by the depot fitter for its photograph to be taken! It looks most attractive in front of the most imposing depot facade, with the sculptured Municipal coat of arms, and its trolley tower is fitted with Illumination decorations for the Autumn Season. Note that the depot has its own flag pole, mounted centrally and reached by ladder. The swivel head of the tram's trolley can reach the overhead from track 7, demonstrating the flexibility of Marton cars. *A. D. Packer*

Visiting its native Bispham Depot during a tour in March 1961 is Box 40 of 1914. The depot provides a fitting setting; over the centre doors is the headstone stating 'Blackpool & Fleetwood Tramroad 1898', since 1920 owned by Blackpool Corporation. The original Tramroad car contrasts with the native Brush cars seen within, now exclusive to Bispham Depot with the Pantographs. Original buildings include a power station, stores and office. *Author*

Blundell Street Depot, with its new entrance from Rigby Road, in 1964, in front of the Transport Office where the staff cars park. Upon the tower-wagon the men are at work fitting the new overhead line, with the impressive depot facade and its title in stone behind them. It is dominated by the gasometer, and the small building beneath it houses the Mayor's limousine, an important neighbour for the trams! *Author*

It is Coronation Day - 21 June 1953 - hence this review of the fleet at Rigby Road Depot, dressed with pendant flags on their trolleys. The fleet livery contrasts between the double-decker Balloons and railcoaches in the wartime green livery, with the Coronations and railcoaches in cream. Certainly some people liked the flare on the front dash of the Streamliners, in cream on green or green on cream. It is noticeable that the Coronations are standing at intervals on the tracks, because of the clearance necessary for their 50-foot length and the resultant overhang at each end. *R. B. Parr, TMS collection*

Looking out from the centre of the depot on 12 September 1959 are trams standing over the pits for inspection. Side by side are Balloons 262 and 259, Coronation 322 and prototype 237, partially in the wartime livery with it upper panels painted cream. They are showing 'DEPOT' on their blinds, although 237 is showing 'CIRCULAR' on one! The works cars can just be seen on the extreme right: Pantograph 167 and Grinder car 1. *Author*

In 1964 Blundell Street Depot has become a store for a variety of trams, seen here on 28 July in a view from Dreadnought 59's top deck. Through the tower of a Boat car can be seen the illuminated car Blackpool Belle, with the Rocket behind. Nearer the doorway are Television trams 166 & 165, with railcoaches 267 & 266 next to them. The depot is also used by the Blackpool ambulances, and the men use the depot offices adjacent to the old doorway. *Author*

A busy scene in Marton Depot on 4 July 1962, with a cleaner washing the front of the school special Balloon 242, while an electrician carries two fluorescent tubes for the modern Marton Vambacs. In the foreground is the 1926 Jubilee illuminated car, stripped of its lights ready for scrapping. Service cars can be seen at the back of the pits on the left, and beyond the central air-raid shelter can be seen the Boat cars and the veteran Standards. *Author*

Bispham Depot is seen here on 27 July 1963 in its last season, with a variety of trams on view. This trio comprises the surviving Marton Vambac 11, the surviving Pantograph 170, used by Permanent Way gang, and a useful Boat car. The height of the ceiling shows how low the trolleys must be bent, having been designed in the days of the Tramroad Company with only single-deckers and no trolley towers mounted on them. The inspection pits run along the length of the tracks. *Author*

The historic Copse Road Depot in Fleetwood on 19 February 1962, showing the yard used for storing permanent way equipment and its two vehicles. The electric locomotive of 1923 was used between 1925 and 1949 for hauling coal wagons from the railway junction at the rear of this depot to Thornton Gate sidings. Pantograph car 170 was used as the track gang's transporter to and from places of track when relaying, and also pulled rail-carrying bogies, seen to its left. The headstone in the apex of the roof reads 'Blackpool & Fleetwood Tramroad 1897'. Although closed in 1963, it remains standing to this day. *Author*

Tram workshops

The Body Shop in 1959, where railcoaches 277 and 272 are being rebuilt as towing cars for the new trailer trams to be delivered in 1960. While the body is retaining its profile, new attractive ends are being built round the driver's cab, facilitating his sitting down to drive and resembling a Coronation car. The resin-bonded fibreglass dome at the end of the roof provides a single large indicator screen. Also in company is 141, the former Progress illuminated car, which is being prepared as a new one - but which was rejected, due to age! *Author*

A general view of the Fitting Shop on 10 April 1964, showing Coronation 319 with its trolley tied down. It is over the inspection pit, which is fitted with a wheel-drop facility. On the centre track stands a pair of bogies under the rail crane, which is able to lift heavy parts like motors and bogie frames. Incidentally, the trams were lifted in the depot and the bogies shunted in here, where they could be cleaned and refitted with new wheel tyres. A row of machinery can be seen, and a blacksmith's forge at the bottom of the workshop, where metal could be shaped. *Author*

Looking into the new Body Shop on the same date, we see Brush cars 286 and 294 being re-panelled and having their sliding sunshine roofs removed to be converted to a fixed roof. Through the windows can be seen three Balloons in the Paint Shop, adjacent to the Body Shop after the Works reorganisation in 1963, when all Works facilities were concentrated in one building. Access to these two workshops was now by shunting trams over a track-fan using a diesel wagon or Engineering car 3. *Author*

Right Pantograph 172, fresh from the Body Shop, stands on board the traverser, which carried trams sideways from the approach track to the various Works Departments. Many tracks led off the traverser pit on each side, between the Body Shops, Fitting Shop and the Paint Shop. The bollard on the corner of the traverser platform and the winch in the middle show how the trams were hauled out of the Works. This traditional method of movement was seen in the London tram depots to improve shunting large numbers, and this example was unique to Blackpool until 1963. *R. P. Fergusson*

Below The Paint Shop in June 1959, where rebuilt Brush car 300 with its new single indicator is being repainted. It is seen with a cream trolley tower, green roof and grey undercoat on the panels. In contrast is the Engineering Overhead Line Car No 4, with the inspection platform raised; the men are repainting it in the all-green Works style. No 4 had been a Works car since 1934 when it ceased to be passenger car 31. However, it is interesting to disclose that today it is once again passenger car 31, at the North of England Open Air Museum at Beamish! *Author*

Works cars and trackwork

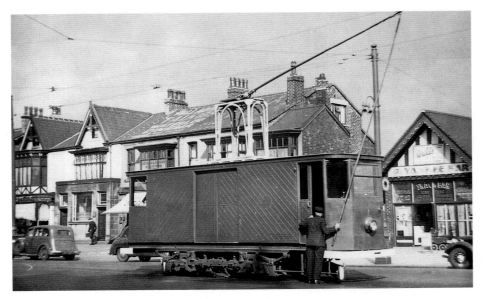

No 1, one of two Grinder cars that dated from 1928, seen here being reversed on the crossover in Lytham Road at the junction with Station Road. They were used to grind the corrugations off the surface of the rail; the track-grinding shoes fitted with carborundum stone, seen between the wheels, were wound down to the track; they were changed as they wore down, and cost £1 each in the Sixties. Inside the car is a water tank, which is drained by pipes in front of the grinding shoes, helping them to slide along the surface. To avoid delaying the service cars, the grinders were sent out at night - and might wake sleepers! *A. D. Packer collection*

The flags are flying in Bispham to celebrate Gala Day in July 1959, a sunny Saturday. Travelling down Red Bank Road is the new Engineering Car 3, rebuilt from Standard 143 in 1958 and capable of running under diesel power in an emergency. It was based at Bispham Depot, and a service car can just be seen turning into the depot yard further down the street. No 3 was able to serve the northern part of the Blackpool & Fleetwood tramway, and act in an emergency from Bispham. *Author*

A scene at the Cabin on 29 July 1963 with Balloon 254 passing the tower-wagon, which has come to supervise men painting the traction poles cream and green - soon to be changed to 'rainbow hues'. In the trilby hat is Mr Wylie - the overhead supervisor - who visits all works and ensures that the ladders are used effectively on their wheeled trolleys. However, you could always escape by taking the Cliff Lift to the Boating Pool below, for a break! *Author*

BLACKPOOL TRAMS 1950-1966

An unusual scene along Whitegate Drive in 1947, with the nearside track being relaid. In the foreground the track gang are excavating the old track, one using a drill to break up the road surface. Level with Standard 144 can be seen new stone foundation and track; the service car is running on the wrong side of the road, but its swivel-head trolley stays in the right place. Bound for SOUTH PIER, 144 was to become the first tram to leave Blackpool for the USA in 1955, and is still in the Seashore Trolley Museum, Maine, to this day. The sign for 'Stanley Park' points down Knowsley Avenue; many people visited the park, travelling by tram. *A. D. Packer*

A scene at Royal Oak and the junction of the Marton and Squires Gate routes during the winter of 1958, when the pointwork was being relaid by the Corporation track gang. While this was taking place the Squires Gate trams were terminating at Manchester Square, and buses were operating along Lytham Road. It is interesting to see how the street surface was excavated to reveal the concrete foundations for the track. However, as new track and pointwork was laid, tar was poured to insulate the steel rail from the hard foundation, making for quieter running for the trams. Red flags warn the motorists and pedestrians, while the track gang have a tea-break! *Author*

By contrast, here is a sunny scene on the Promenade at Whitsuntide 1965, when the track gang are getting sunburned while dealing with the crossover at Princess Parade. They have lifted the flags with their picks, and dug out the sand to gain access to the sleepers. In the path of the halted railcoach a workman is tightening a joint in the track, while Balloon 260 heads for Bispham. The wagon parked at the roadside contains the welding equipment, used to weld the joints when complete. What a pleasant job! *Author*

We're off! This is the scene at Pleasure Beach loop on 10 April 1964, where 271 has left the track and demolished the railings with its rear-end. This adds to the interesting sights for the man sitting on the rocks and the little children watching nearby. Chief Engineer Eric Kay surveys the marks of the wheels upon the flagstones, and wonders if the tram came round the corner too fast on its way to Fleetwood. *Author*

What is the driver looking for through the windscreen of his service Coronation, stopped at Manchester Square? This tram seems to be trying to do the impossible - OXFORD in Marton - on 28 July 1963! However, he may have operated the points for Lytham Road when really he is on a Promenade service for Starr Gate. This unusual situation is watched by the passengers of passing Boat car 227, and on the upper deck of the Dreadnought behind him. Yes, it is Daily Mirror Week in Blackpool! *Author*

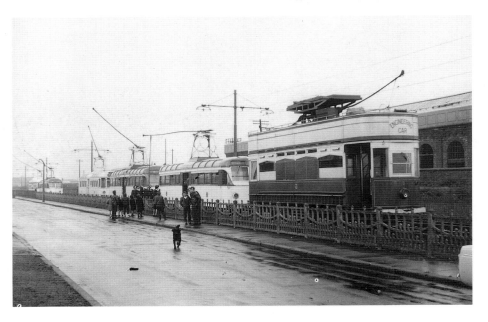

Here's a sight at the Engine Sheds, Radcliffe Road, Fleetwood, at 8.10 pm on 7 May 1962, as the locals watch the trams with their trolleys in the air - and a dog comes to meet the photographer! There is a stoppage because all the power has been lost, so the trolleys of 280, 286 and 271 have been disconnected and the Engineering Car has travelled powered by its diesel engine. If it raises its trolley it can generate power and feed into the overhead - but not push all three trams together. What next? *Author*

. . . scrappings and an escape

The scene at Thornton Gate at Easter 1958, as three of the old Standard cars - 42, 28 and 177 - are in three stages of scrapping - what a tragedy! During the winter six Standards were towed from Marton Depot and lined up on the siding. This was an unusual sight for passengers to see from the service trams in this location. *Author*

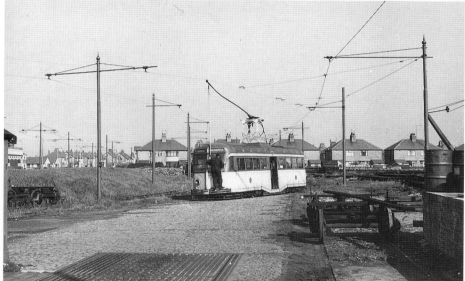

The same location on Friday 20 September 1963, as railcoach 201 is driven across the siding to the far corner, with a man riding on the fender holding the trolley pole. This tram is now 'RESERVED' for the scrap-merchant. That morning 201 was travelling to North Station on route 10 when it was stopped at Bispham, its passengers transferred to Brush car 300, and then driven here. What a fate! Its trolley was lifted off the overhead, and its cable cut ready for its certain demise. *Author*

However, a tram can escape from Blackpool, as Coronation 327 proves, seen here travelling by wagon to Lytham Railway Museum on 18 August 1976. After getting soaked by a flood of the tide there, it went on to Southport Steamport, and is now in Bradford, West Yorkshire, Museum - where it may run again one day! *Author*

Preservation - National Tramway Museum UK and San Francisco USA

Above left The arrival of the two 40s at Crich, Derbyshire, on 5 October 1963, where the crane first lifts Standard 40 from the low-loader and places it on its bogies, as the members push for guidance. The 40 was then pushed to the depot, and the crane unloaded Box 40. Blackpool's famous trams thus joined the National Collection. *Author*

Left A view of the Tramway Museum on 20 June 1964, and Box 40 is travelling under power along the main line towards Town End. The spire of Crich parish church can be seen in the village where the TMS bought this site to develop as the Tramway Museum. No 40 passes several tram trucks and bogies and Glasgow Cunarder 1297, protected by canvas. Interestingly 1297 visited Blackpool in 1985, and 40 returned in 1988. *Author*

Top In March 1965 Dreadnought 59 left Blackpool and became popular at the National Tramway Museum; it is seen here on the main line. The dramatic Crich Stand - above the quarry face - provides a very different environment from the seaside! However, 59 did return to Blackpool from 1975 to 1990. *A. D. Packer collection*

Left Standard 40, apparently destined for PLEASURE BEACH, is in fact heading for Cliffeside on a members' day at Crich in 1966, followed by Glasgow 812 and B&F crossbench car 2. Behind the tram can be seen an antiques fair on the top of the embankment, and a worker balancing on the traction pole bracket arm. Incidentally 40 returned to Blackpool for the Centenary in 1985. *A. D. Packer collection*

Twenty-two Blackpool trams are preserved, six of them in the USA, and the most remarkable is Boat car 228 operated by MUNI in San Francisco. It is seen here in Market Street, the busy city centre, where the Trolley Festival operates for the benefit of tourists and citizens. MUNI have collected an international tram fleet, and asked Blackpool for an open Boat car as an unusual addition. In 1985 Blackpool sent 228, the most travelled international tram, having been loaned to Philadelphia for operation in 1976, and subsequently returned!

Right and below Here in Market Street passengers enjoy sitting in the sunshine for their sightseeing ride on the open Boat car. It was a novelty for me to be destined for PLEASURE BEACH VIA PROMENADE - certainly the unique tram became very full at peak periods, when the citizens preferred riding on the trams rather than the Subway. *Author*

Bottom The international image is established in this scene, as Blackpool Boat 228 is passed in Market Street by Oporto 189 from Portugal, itself followed by a police car. *Author*

Below right In the suburb of Castro the Blackpool Boat is reversed round the corner past the Grocery Liquor store to the terminus. The passengers have a mystery ride backwards! You may notice the national Stars & Stripes and Union Jack flags flying from the corner pillars, and, from the trolley rope, the Skull & Crossbones - for an international Boat! *Author*

Snow in the suburbs

Snow is very rare upon the Blackpool & Fleetwood Tramroad, but is seen here on 28 December 1964 - how it changes the scene!

Left Brush car 291 passes Rossall Farm, concealed by its white embankment, and looks quite picturesque on its snowy reservation. The passing lorry on Broadway is silenced by the frosty atmosphere. *Author*

Middle left Coronation 310 passes through the wilderness at Thornton Gate, but the tram track is clear - possibly the tramway snowplough has kept it clear. *Author*

Bottom left People walk on the snowy cliffs at Bispham while railcoach 271 journeys north into the mist. However, passengers can gain comfort from the Methodist Church's sign - 'You are welcome'. *Author*

Below Bound for Fleetwood, the dark profile of 290 rounds the corner at the farm crossing opposite Rossall School grounds. Fortunately, heaters have been fitted in the saloons of winter service cars. *Author*

BLACKPOOL TRAMS 1950-1966